STEP-
T

STEP-BY-STEP
TAROT

A COMPLETE COURSE IN TAROT READERSHIP

Terry Donaldson

Thorsons
An Imprint of HarperCollins*Publishers*

Thorsons
An Imprint of HarperCollins*Publishers*
77–85 Fulham Palace Road
Hammersmith, London W6 8JB
1160 Battery Street
San Francisco, California 94111–1213

Published by Thorsons 1995

10 9 8 7 6 5 4 3 2 1

© Terry Donaldson 1995

Terry Donaldson asserts the moral right to
be identified as the author of this work

A catalogue record for this book
is available from the British Library

ISBN 1 85538 431 0

Printed in Great Britain by
Woolnough Bookbinding Ltd.,
Irthlingborough, Northants

CONTENTS

ACKNOWLEDGEMENTS

Many thanks to the following people for their support, ideas and contributions which have made this book possible:

To Dan Fletcher of Cartoon Box, 102 Silverleigh Road, Thornton Heath, Surrey, for the pictures; Evelyne Herbin for her guidance; Steven Bickler for his eye for detail and going through the proofs till 2 a.m.; Vivi Cohen for the auditing; Diana Clifton for the yoga; Peter Pracownik and Jazz Deville with whom I have been working on the forthcoming Dragon Tarot deck and the dragon game 'Wyvern', both published by U.S. Games Systems, Inc.; Stuart Kaplan, President of U.S. Games Systems, Inc., for his sense of vision; Fiona Brown, my editor, and Peter and Freya, for their patience.

To all my teachers and all my students,
especially to Evelyne
who has somehow succeeded in playing
both roles.

INTRODUCTION AND HISTORICAL ORIGINS

WHAT YOU WILL ACCOMPLISH

There have been many books on the Tarot, but never one like this.

This book has come into existence as a result of my training other people in the field of Tarot readership, of having trained personally over 1,000 people in the subject to a high standard, in many countries and in many languages, and on a one-to-one basis over a 20-year period.

The techniques which I am giving you in this manual are techniques which I know work, and, if you follow them through, will enable you to experience the wonder which the Tarot holds in store for you.

The experience of Tarot readership is not a trivial one. To desire to work with the Tarot, whether to be able to do readings and to help other people or even for one's own insight into the meaning of life is a really enjoyable thing to be able to do!

HOW THE TAROT CAN HELP

The Tarot has always held a great deal of mystery down through the ages, especially for those who have desired to become more familiar with its message.

It is a message – or a map – of how we may achieve greater fulfil-ment in our lives, through a balancing of the emotional aspects with the material. Not through a denial of either. Many people can't see a way out of their problems because they do not have an alternative point of reference from which they can begin to see what choices they do have. The Tarot reading can be that starting-point for many.

It is important that the Tarot reading is well delivered. It is not enough just to say things off the top of one's head in the hope that maybe some of it will stick or somehow make sense to the Querent. (A 'Querent' is someone who has come to ask a question

1

from the Tarot.) It is also important that the reader is able to work directly from the imagery of the cards, without having to disturb the continuity of the reading by breaking off to get out a book to check on the meanings of cards.

There is an intellectual discipline involved in learning how to read the Tarot, just as there was a discipline involved in first learning how to read the words which you are looking at now. But it is not a difficult one. There is a sensitivity involved in the art of reading the Tarot. It is not a mechanical process either. You could say that it is a bit similar to learning a craft.

MISGUIDED NOTIONS

There are people out there who still cling to the outdated notion that to be able to read the Tarot you have to be born with a hereditary gift to do so; that the art of Tarot reading is something akin to having dimples or buck teeth: it would have to come down the family line.

The truth is that the door of the Tarot opens itself to all those who genuinely desire to understand its mysteries, and who would make positive use of the knowledge and guidance which they would receive.

The exercises which I am giving you have enabled many people from many different backgrounds, religions, walks of life and educational levels to make sense of the imagery of the Tarot, and to become skilled and effective readers for social, personal and professional purposes.

I have had many professional readers come by to train with me and without exception they have all gained greatly from the experience. I have their feedback letters on my noticeboard for anyone who is interested to come by and look at.

For a long time I was very resistant to the idea of writing up the set of training exercises and making them available indiscriminately to the public. I used to have a very set idea that the Tarot could really only be taught in a one-to-one student/teacher ratio. The Tarot today is being promoted through workshops, weekend courses, correspondence courses, even holidays abroad, as well as in its historical tradition of one-to-one.

THE NEED TODAY

Now more than ever there is a real need for people to think in terms of getting themselves trained as readers, so that they can be effective in giving guidance to the many out there in our society who need it, who are seeking. So that they can be instrumental in guiding themselves as well!

The wonderful thing is that in the Tarot, there's something for everyone! The basic message of the Tarot is that there is hope and that such hope may be realized through creative change.

In the pictures of the Tarot we have a set of windows through which we may look at life. We have a description of how the mighty creative forces of the universe ebb and flow, of how Yin and Yang manifest their energies in a physical world.

Compressed in the cards, we have many legends and stories from mythologies, astrological and archetypal significance, and esoteric secrets from a wide range of backgrounds.

FINGERS POINTING TO THE MOON

But they are all different fingers pointing to the same moon: hints as to the kind of perceptions we first need to make in order to be able to change our lives. In other words, we all see the same truths from a different viewpoint.

Thus the meanings of the Tarot cards will actually change for you over time. As you grow and develop as a being, so your own needs will evolve and so, therefore, what you see taking place in the Tarot imagery will go through transformation.

HISTORICAL ORIGINS

As to the historical origins of the Tarot, there are many different explanations. The actual Tarot as we know it today dates back to fourteenth-century Italy where we find a nobleman commissioning a hand-painted deck to commemorate the marriage of his daughter. But there are historical records to indicate the use of cards for divinatory purposes earlier than that.

We have always used symbols, in one form or another. Indeed, it is where we get the letters of the alphabet from, each of which at one time held a particular meaning. The Runestones, the Ogham, etc, all date back a lot further than the Tarot as such, although in one sense we might regard them as the earliest forms of Tarot, with their straight lines being marked on pieces of wood or stone to represent storm, harvest, war, protection, etc.

It is from the casting down onto the ground of these stones in ancient times that we have the phrase 'magic spell', because from the single letters which would be carved on each individual stone, the local 'wise person' would be able to spell (i.e. make out) the words or utterances of the gods which they believed protected them.

The word 'magic' is from the same root as the words 'image', 'imagination', 'magi'. It is therefore pointing us in the direction of achieving wisdom, through the development of our ability to creatively visualize, to imagine. To put aside your preconceived notions, to let your intuition function with less restraint from your conscious mind, to become aware of your own limitations and to move increasingly beyond them.

This is the very essence of how to approach the Tarot.

LOOK NO FURTHER

One thing I would ask of you before we begin this course: put aside any other books which you have on the subject, books you have already tried to work with. If you go to one doctor for a course of treatment, it would be inappropriate to continue taking medicine from other prescribers.

You will find all you need to learn the art of Tarot readership here in THIS course. I mean it. After you have completed it, you can then go back to all of those other books and you will then get 10 times more from them than you would ever have done before.

1

EFFORTLESS EFFORT

You will master the Tarot not by struggling with 'the meanings' or by battling with the cards in any sense whatsoever.

Sometimes it may be that you hit an impasse in your studies.

Don't panic. Nothing is accomplished without sacrifice, perseverance and patience.

And the sacred mysteries don't always reveal themselves to the casual enquirer.

You will make progress in your studies if you can allow yourself to *enjoy* what you are doing.

And by exercising the principle of *effortless effort*.

This is not the principle of laziness, though, but of gently, effortlessly, *stretching* into the work which lies before you!

2

A DECK YOU WILL BE COMFORTABLE WITH

One of the most important matters in the first stages of your Tarot quest is the selection of the deck which you are going to work with.

A few words of warning on this.

It could be that someone has walked into a bookshop and bought you a deck of cards already; or passed on to you the cards which were used by their great aunt back in the nineteenth century.

There are many different kinds of Tarot decks out there. Some are oriented towards specific sets of legends, e.g. Greek, Egyptian, Arthurian. And unless you are familiar with those sets of legends already, you are going to have to handle two sets of learning: the principles of Tarot readership on the one hand *and* the belief system or symbolic system contained within the deck's imagery.

There are many decks in which the Minor Arcana are shown not by any picture, but by what we call 'pip' symbols, e.g. sets of swords crossed over each other, or rows of cups lined up against each other. But to learn from these decks is going to involve a *great* deal of memory work as well.

Another category to avoid would be decks which are heavily laden with huge quantities of symbolism, magic, astrology, alchemy, etc. The reason again is obvious: far too much to take in all at once.

Once you have a solid basis to work from, you will find that bit by bit all these other weird and wonderful decks start opening themselves up to you. But until you have a really solid foundation, leave them well alone.

It is important that you select your own deck, so this will entail going alone to a bookshop that specializes in Tarot decks and looking at the portfolio which they will invariably have. Here, you can look through a vast selection of different decks, with all the cards held behind a sheet of transparent film.

Ask for some guidance from the assistant if you are unsure and don't be afraid to say that you are just starting out on the road of readership. You will find that they may well have a recommendation to make.

Probably the best decks to work from as you learn the Tarot are the Ryder-Waite and Morgan-Greer decks. But in the end it will have to be your own choice.

As you progress in your studies, it is very likely that you will build up your own collection of different decks and will have them out on the table when people come for readings, so that as you begin the session, you will be able to ask which deck they would like you to read from.

If you have already selected a deck for yourself or feel drawn to work with the deck you have, then fine. This is going to be the one for you!

All you have to do now is to follow the training steps and we'll be turning you into a reader!

3
HOW THE TAROT WORKS

The Tarot is something which functions on many levels.

On one level, it is a set of cards which portray a way of looking at the world. A way of making sense of the world, rather than an attempt to define and limit it.

On another level, it is an approach to life, which enables each of us to move away from our own private realities towards the point of being able to have a *multi-viewpoint*.

A lot of top-level executives these days are finding themselves on expensive courses which attempt to nudge them out of their own personal mind-set and develop qualities of mental flexibility and creativity. This was – and is – the first and primary purpose of the Tarot: to give us a set of windows through which we can look upon life. It has other qualities too:

It is a counselling tool.
It is a means through which communication – sometimes on a
    highly psychic or intuitive level – can take place.
It is the means through which countless people over countless
    years have found a place to gain a resolution to the problems
    which have beset them.

The Tarot works through synchronicity – in other words, the random patterns in which the cards seem to fall are part of a greater pattern within the cosmic scheme of things. This may seem chaotic to some, but not to those who seek to understand the nature of the causes of things; to those who have learned to look for causes which in turn give rise to effects.

This, then, is the function of the Tarot: to facilitate our grasp of how things may be changed in the future through a deepening of our realization of what has happened in the past.

As a trainee, you are entering a new doorway.

May your life never be the same again!

4

STORY-TELLING WITH THE TAROT

THE BARDIC TECHNIQUE

Once you have worked with this you will be able to open up a lot of modern fiction, especially fantasy, sword and sorcery books, and see how their authors actually did it! I actually know a number of writers who use this technique whenever they get stuck for some inspiration.

We are going to use it because it gets you to the point of working more intuitively and imaginatively with the images on a set of cards, without wondering how right or wrong you might be.

What you must do here is lay out a set of, say, three or four cards. That will be enough for the moment. When you get the hang of it, you might well want to lay out sets and rows of them.

Now, without even trying to remember 'what they mean', *make up a story – a simple little children's story or a fairy story –* using the pictures on the row of cards as a source of inspiration.

It's a lot simpler, I have found, for those that already have children, as they often get asked for stories at bedtime.

But even if you don't have children, it is still part of your initiation to develop your story-telling technique. In the ancient Druid Order (and I believe the same still applies today), the first grade of initiation was that of the bard, the story-teller, whose role it would be to entertain, to enlighten, to teach, using songs and poetry, music and legends, in order to do so. They would travel around the land, teaching and learning as they went.

On the facing page, I have given you an example.

Just below, I have chosen for you at random the Knight of Wands, the Seven of Wands, the Ace of Coins and the King of Swords.

It isn't a bad idea actually to use the words 'Once upon a time...' in starting off. Somehow it seems to set the little story up just right.

KNIGHT OF WANDS (RODS)

Once upon a time, there was a Knight of the Round Table, who became severely disillusioned with how his life was going. He wasn't even sure what changes he wanted to make; all he knew was that he wanted to do some travelling.

SEVEN OF WANDS

One day he was travelling around the countryside when suddenly he saw a band of brigands setting upon a single traveller, attempting to rob him. The Knight went straight to the man's rescue, and although the brigands didn't run off immediately, they didn't put up too much resistance either.

ACE OF COINS (PENTACLES)

The traveller was greatly relieved to have received such assistance and gave the knight a coin with a special symbol engraved upon it.

'Take it,' he said, 'and if ever you find yourself in the city of

Hyperborea, give it to the Sheriff, who will know what to do with it.'

The Knight took the coin, took his leave and set off on his journey, and one day he arrived at the city of Hyperborea, famous for the great arch which marked the entrance to the city's gates.

THE KING OF SWORDS

While the Knight was there, he got into some trouble and was hauled up before the city's Sheriff. The Sheriff was known to be a very severe judge in these matters, but the Knight showed him the special coin and instead of being punished, he was welcomed into the Sheriff's own household that very night.

As you can see, this kind of story could go on for ever and ever! But it is interesting to set the cards out in this way and just to let your imagination do the work.

The point of doing lots and lots of work on the story-telling technique is that it starts to exercise the muscles of your imagination. As this starts to grow, so does your ability to 'tune in' to what is going on in the life of the person in front of you.

Your imaginative faculty is what is going to be doing 90 per cent of the work in any reading. It is this – and this alone – which makes the difference between a mechanistic recital of the cards and a lively, living, breathing experience out of which your Querent is going to emerge suitably impressed. You don't have to write these stories down. You can just let them run in your head, picking cards at random and letting them trigger imaginative tales that don't have to lead anywhere in particular. You don't have to make a big deal out of this. You can even take the cards out on the way to work on a bus or a train and go through them there.

5

TAROT WORKSHEETS

You might like to copy the sheet entitled 'Tarot Worksheet' (see page 14) and create a complete page for each of the cards, 78 in all. At this stage, I want you to start building up your selection of associated memories and experiences for each of the cards. I want you, when you look at any one card, to reach the point of being able to link the picture with a complete set of feelings, memories, recollections, etc. It is this attribute which makes a great Tarot reading. Once you have worked through the deck in this way, your readings will not just be two-dimensional recitals of 'the meaning of the cards', in the way that so many self-trained people's readings are. They will actually resonate with emotional intensity; they will become *three*-dimensional. *They will acquire depth.*

The actual exercise is simple: take each card and place it on a Worksheet. Now allow your thoughts to flow around the images which surface in your mind as you look at it. As they start to appear I want you to quickly write down all the associations which come up.

There will be memories of people, places, experiences positive and negative. *Be specific: name names, put down times when things happened. Be as specific as you can.* The more accurately you can do this, the more you will be genuinely weaving your own life experience into the symbolism of the cards.

Thoughts, hopes, dreams, ambitions, fears, desires will be triggered as you do this, making associations and connections with each card. Sometimes some of the experiences you will be reminded of will not be happy ones, but in doing this exercise you will be clearing emotional debris out of your system. Better out than in!

The whole purpose of the Worksheets is to act quickly, to get the immediate psychological response which the image of each card triggers off, before the critical faculty has a chance to step in and create a blockage.

It is a good idea to cycle through the Worksheets, going through them fairly quickly at first, and then come back to them when you feel ready. Each time you go through a card, you will get something more from the exercise.

There will be some cards from which you get more than from others. Some will have a lot to say to you; others will have their say with you further along your path. Some of the experiences which come back to you will be very intense. With some of them you may laugh, with others you may well cry.

But to work with the Tarot is to work on yourself, in the sense of looking at your own limitations, your own blockages, and finding a way to clear them. After all, unless you've cleared these away for yourself, at least to some extent, how can you realistically expect to help others to do so?

You will notice that the sheet entitled 'Neighbouring Page' (see page 15) gives you the chance to write up all of your own more intimate and detailed reactions to the specific memories thrown up by each of the cards as you move through this set of exercises. The more you put into these exercises, the more you will actively participate in your own growth process.

Feel free to write up any residual emotions, regrets, realizations, hopes for the future, aspirations which you now have. Remember, you don't have to show them to anyone.

We don't often get the chance in life to actually sit down and talk much to ourselves, to simply sit there and *be*, and get into

TAROT WORKSHEET

Memories?   Desires?

Place the
Tarot card
here

Hopes?   Fears?

Plans?

NEIGHBOURING PAGE

What happened here?

Where?   When?
Why?   With who?   How?

What did you learn from this experience?

What has this card to teach you?

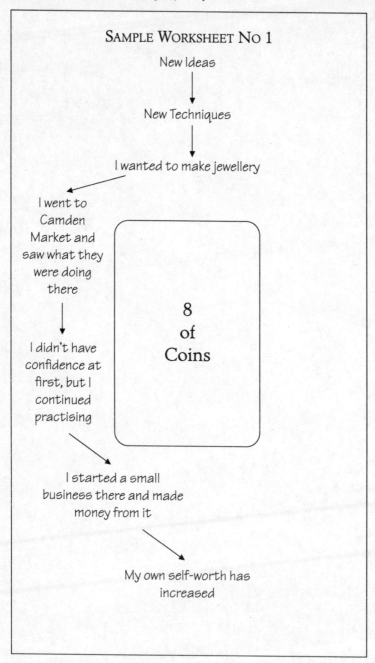

SAMPLE WORKSHEET No 1

New Ideas

New Techniques

I wanted to make jewellery

I went to
Camden
Market and
saw what they
were doing
there

8
of
Coins

I didn't have
confidence at
first, but I
continued
practising

I started a small
business there and made
money from it

My own self-worth has
increased

SAMPLE WORKSHEET NO 2

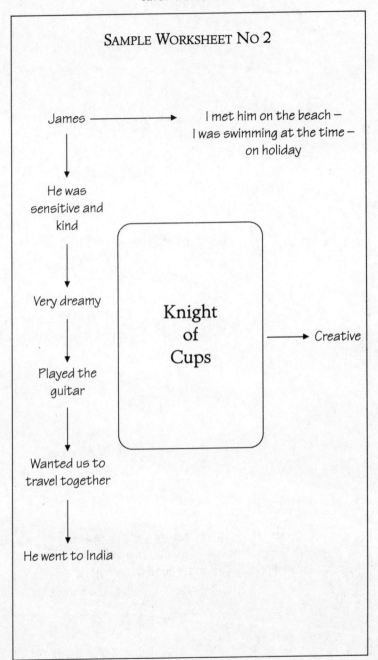

James ⟶ I met him on the beach –
I was swimming at the time –
on holiday

He was
sensitive and
kind

Very dreamy

Knight
of
Cups ⟶ Creative

Played the
guitar

Wanted us to
travel together

He went to India

Sample Worksheet No 3

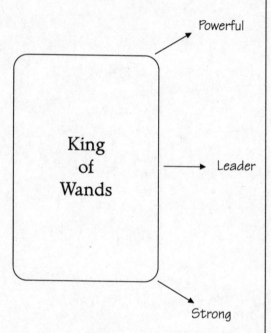

Dynamic

Powerful

King
of
Wands

Leader

Strong

Reminds me of Steve when he won the race —
Everyone came out to meet him and he led
the big celebration through the village

SAMPLE WORKSHEET NO 4

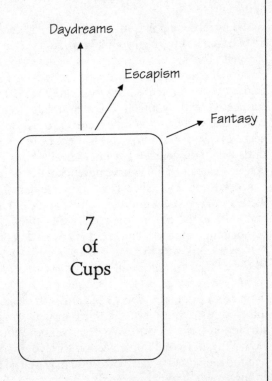

Daydreams

Escapism

Fantasy

7
of
Cups

Time: July '89 – November '90

I was confused about my life in general – I was
bored and taking tranquillisers – I was getting out
of it – I felt it was an effort to get up in the
morning. Then, my daughter had an accident and I
realised how precious she was to me. Suddenly I
was able to snap out of it: I stopped taking the
pills and regained control over my life

communication with our emotions and thoughts. All the time we are rushing from one sensory experience to another. Sitting down and working your way through the Worksheets is a wonderful chance to befriend yourself, to heal yourself of old wounds, and to determine and prepare for those things that you want to find in life in the future.

The purpose of going through the Worksheets is two-fold. The first I have already given you: it gets you much more in touch with yourself. The second is that it enables you to make more of an emotional connection with the person who is having their cards read. You are far more able to connect with them if you have connected with yourself first. To relate to someone on an emotional level is not an intellectual process. It is a matter of the heart. In a very real sense you will not be able to see in anyone's cards what you yourself have not already been through. You will not see heartbreak if you have never experienced it.

Keep all your Worksheets in a special folder after you have done them and keep them in order, so that you can refer back to them and add extra pages on each card, thus building up the compendium of associated experience for each one.

It is very important that you thoroughly personalize each individual Worksheet for each individual card. We must get all the details of the specific experience or memory associated with each card, locating it all in time and space, with where, when and with whom. It is *not* enough that you just write down the 'meaning' or any other superficial attribution for each card. What we want is Who, Where, When, How, Why and What in connection with your most personal (and painful) memories for each card. You may well go through bouts of crying, anger, happiness, etc. But write down the details of each of these memories. To work with the Tarot in this way is soul-cleansing and therapeutic. Also, you will access a different realm of insight into what the cards are hinting at in each of your Querent's spreads when you have tapped into the true emotional, gritty meaning of each card and how it is linked with your own emotional past.

Also make a point of writing down any cognitions, thoughts, realizations, hopes, fears, prayers for absent friends, etc. which emerge from these exercises. Again, don't make a big deal out of these exercises. Get through them so that you can go beyond them. You can always come back to them and redo them. If you find yourself spending more than 10 minutes on any card, go on to the next one. Keep all your notes intact and in order. Write at the top of each Worksheet the name of the card you were looking at when you did the write-up, so that you don't get them mixed up.

You share karma with the person in front of you. Therefore, by tapping into your own emotional reservoir of experience, you will be able to 'see' 1,000 times more things going on in your Querent's cards than you would have otherwise. This is a powerful technique, but to get the benefit of it you have to go deeply into yourself and the experiences in life which you have felt. It takes guts. But you will end up a far more effective reader if you do it than if you don't.

6

THE HEIGHTENED MEANINGS

ABOUT THE HEIGHTENED MEANINGS

Here I am going to fill you in on some of the meanings of the cards. They are all oriented towards relating the meanings of each card to practical aspects of life and try to move beyond the simplistic meanings which you will find in the little booklets accompanying each deck. By the same token, they also try to get you thinking about the issues which are raised and to enable the Querent to become a little more determined by the end of the reading.

These meanings are more empowering than some of the esoteric waffle found in certain sources.

The Heightened Meanings have been written not with a view to making any definitive statement on the meanings of each card, but rather to get you as a trainee thinking along new lines. So some of the meanings you will agree with more than others. But I don't want you to get stuck at agreement or disagreement. I want you to continue to develop your own associations, using the Heightened Meanings as a guide for your own continued work.

As you go through this chapter, why not keep a notebook beside you, so that you can write up your own Heightened Meanings, card by card.

You will notice that I have only given you these meanings *after* you have gone through the Worksheets and other exercises. The meanings you have derived for yourself do not have to match up exactly with the Heightened Meanings. To some extent there should be a basic consensus, because the Tarot is based around a pattern, but within that very wide pattern is the potential for an infinite number of personalizations.

So there is no sense of 'getting it wrong', really; only of weaving the symbolism which the Tarot has to offer into the context of your own life.

THE MAJOR ARCANA

0 THE FOOL

Encounters with other people will become very lively indeed! The kind of people you are meeting are outside the realm of what has gone on before. You will be experiencing them as interesting, exciting, enlivening! You will be having the same effect on them, by the way, just in case you thought it was a one-way street!

New relationships may take place which will be totally different from anything you have experienced before! Don't go into this new world with all your old knowledge – leave your shoes and your mind by the door! It is only by removing the barrier of existing knowledge that you will be able to receive fresh inflows of teaching, which will pave the way for you to go on to the next level of spiritual development.

It may well be that under this influence you are attracting people who are very different from your normal circle of friends and associates. These new associations may tend to have an unusual quality which makes your existing friends wonder about the direction in life which you are taking. Let them sit and wonder – maybe one day they may even find out!

The whole emphasis is upon freedom, spontaneity, the unusual and that which has the capacity to interest.

If it is essential for you to make any important decisions, especially those which might require long-term commitments, then this isn't the best set of influences. It is far better to postpone these decisions until a time in the future when the correct balance – or at the very least a new balance of the mind's faculties – can be achieved. In particular, steer clear of business decisions, matters involving finances, property, the drawing up of leases or any legal agreements which would be binding or have long-term effects.

This card would certainly point the way towards the development of new skills, new techniques, new abilities. The only problem here is that under this card's influence, it might be difficult to focus the mind or to concentrate on one thing at a time sufficiently to achieve anything concrete. But this would probably be the crux of the whole matter.

It symbolizes a brilliant time for pushing ahead with new plans and projects, although there is in this card a far greater degree of the element of 'experiment' than is to be found anywhere else. Let's not get too disillusioned or upset if some of these experiments don't necessarily work out or at least yield the kind of tangible results which we had originally anticipated!

The Fool is all about the experimental, the original, the eccentric, the different. He is all about not following any pattern at all, just doing his own thing! He is no respecter of outward appearances, but is able to see right to the heart of the other person – or situation – and judge truly. He is a great idealist and by his refusal to compromise himself with the material world he inhabits a rather different dimension. Time, place: neither of these have much effect on him; he is only just in his own body. If he went any higher, he'd slip out of his physical form and go back to the realm of pure spirit. He is a great teacher, but wouldn't want you around for too long, hanging on his every word. He's not here to let you slip out of your self-imposed responsibilities and start projecting onto him. He's not a guru, just his own true self. In the past, he was associated with the element Air, as that was the lightest of all the elements, like the wind, blowing wherever it wanted to blow. More recently, he has been seen in the company of the planet Uranus, which alone out of all the planets in the Solar System rotates horizontally on its axis, going around the Zodiac. So, he is equally eccentric, rotating around the universe in his own original way as well!

He is a breath of fresh air, in a world where orthodoxy has gone mad. Others inevitably copy him, which is where the merchandizing comes in, and the fashion designers, starved of fresh ideas, start seeing new possibilities.

His is the flash of genius which comes like a bolt of lightning: the invention of the paper clip; the rubber band; the milk carton; these are some of his ideas! To hell with 9–5! Who needs all that slavery when you can have a ball?

What could you be doing instead of reading this book? How could you get to meet the Fool? What would you say to him?

1 THE MAGICIAN

In this card you are shown possessing great power, as if a great force were flowing through you, coming in from some higher plane of inspiration and manifesting more fully in your everyday life as energy, action and power. Quite possibly you haven't got yourself fully connected to this great force – as yet. The Magician is here to show you how to!

This card looks at the role of communication, especially to a much wider audience than that to which you are used. You are being described in this card as an intermediary, as if you are in some way the representative of a message which is flowing in from outside and beyond yourself, into action.

This card talks of learning, teaching and intellectual knowledge. It is in these areas, this card is saying, that your next stage of growth is likely. You may well find yourself in the role of teaching, or of learning from others, or both!

The Magician is saying that in the coming period you will be using your knowledge to influence the minds of others. There may even be very specific points of contact between you and those in the advertising industry, media or other branches of the communication industry.

The Magician represents the principle of reason; of thinking things through; of talking with others and consulting them on their viewpoints. He likes libraries, which to him are symbols of tremendous work done by mighty minds. He is able to look at a book and know just how much work has gone into it, how many years of collecting data, collating it, digesting it and then displaying it so that someone else can share in that knowledge. He likes to visit laboratories, where he can give hints as to how new life-saving discoveries can be made, which will help humanity wipe out diseases such as typhoid, smallpox, syphilis and leprosy. He is helpful to those who wish to roll back the borders of human knowledge. All explorers know something of him. All discoverers, too. He is master of communication and can speak all languages. He rules over all education, by which means alone we are rendered fit members of society. Negative aspects of him are shown in mythology when he appears a Loki, the trickster, or as a deceiver or beguiler in some way. Negative aspects of him in life are the confidence trickster, the card sharp, the loan shark. Even more negative would be when he invents something like a new disease or drugs with horrendous side-effects.

The Magician is also master of travel. The Greeks and Romans venerated him as Hermes and Mercury respectively. One of his most important attributes was that of ruling over trade, travel and commerce. His assistance was always invoked at the beginning of any major journey or transaction.

What could you be doing in your life to continue your education? Why not get along to your local library – maybe you haven't been there for some time! Take time out to learn that language you always wanted to brush up on. On another level, what messages are you sending out to others at this time? Are you sure that the messages you are actually sending are the ones that you intend? If not, this could lead to some confusion between you and others, could it not? How could you then ensure that you are going to be better understood? Similarly, how sure are you that you are reading other people's signals properly? For example, do you know about body language, about all of the physical signals which people give off, without any words ever being spoken? Can you tell when someone really likes you and when they don't? Or when they are telling you the truth and when they aren't? This could be something else for you to learn, couldn't it?

The symbol here shows how our own psychic intuition is the most powerful way in which the symbolic veil separating our conscious minds from the collective mind of humanity may be attained. In the inner depths of your own mind, this card is saying, you will find the knowledge that you seek. You must be guided by your own intuition, but not by mere emotional whim, which is not the same thing at all.

Seek within your own past experience the answer to the problem with which you are currently faced: somewhere back there you have been in pretty much the same situation as you are in now.

In this card, you are shown with your feet standing on the Moon, which is a symbol of the mirror of Hathor, the ancient Egyptian goddess of the night sky. This mirror is indicating the need to reflect upon what has happened up until now and the answer will float into the surface level of your mind.

The High Priestess is suppressed in this society, as she is in virtually the whole world at this time. She is the wise woman, who knows without lots of schooling. She has more wisdom and insight in her little finger than most men have in their entire heads. Hers is the ability to use foresight, and to make problems vanish before they grow and multiply. With her insight, we would be able to eradicate the problems of crime without massive expenditures on repressive measures which do nothing to punish the offender, to make him desire change or which give recompense to the victim. With more of her insight, we would be able to find solutions to problems that would completely bypass the 'us versus them' approach which characterizes so much of male-dominated society.

The High Priestess stands there, able and willing to guide us through the labyrinth of our own subconscious minds to the point where we can tap into our higher consciousness and begin to remold our own lives. But we must become more willing to be guided by our own intuition.

3 THE EMPRESS

This card is showing that at this point the way forward for you is to develop and put to use your own creativity, your own ability to make things grow.

We are shown here a representation of Venus, resting in her garden, allowing all the plants and creatures which she has brought into being there with her life-bringing force to grow stronger and take their place in existence. It is a message to you that you also have the ability to create, to bring into existence new things.

You may, for instance, have an artistic ability or sensitivity. If so, then now is the time to put it to use and increase output of whatever is your particular artistic skill.

If you paint, then create many paintings and promote yourself by holding an exhibition in your area. If your sensitivity runs in another direction, then locate it and consciously enhance that.

If you are a woman, this card can indicate that you are going through a period of exceptional fertility and that if you do not want to have a child, then you should take extra steps to ensure that you do not become pregnant.

This card also indicates that the harmonious quality of the planet Venus, which this card represents, is bringing into your life a very peaceful effect – you will observe that contacts with others flow more easily than before.

The Empress rules over our own personal creativity. This card comes up a lot for artists, musicians, actors and actresses. It is directly related to the emotions in which this creative potential is rooted. Without our ability to feel, to experience the different emotions of love, pain, fulfilment and rejection, we are as dead as doornails, at least as far as the Empress is concerned. Many people walk around in life like zombies, blocking themselves off from their own emotions with drugs, alcohol or just with their own insensitivity. The real challenge for them is to learn to accept all of their feelings. This isn't necessarily an easy business. The entire industry of therapy and self-development has boomed over the last couple of decades, designed to help people do just this.

We live in a society in which the Empress is heavily repressed. Our culture is now so TV-based, we all of us, like robots, switch on these machines when we come in – and many of us remain thus transfixed all night. Before the advent of TV and radio, people would learn how to play musical instruments, to sing, to dance together. They would hold plays in the village hall just to entertain themselves. These are all Empress activities.

How would you like to learn how to play an instrument, to dance, to express yourself more fluidly? What about that book you've always wanted to write? Those poems, that play? What about that baby you keep thinking of having? Well, when are you going to switch off the TV and radio and make a start?

Make this the year in which you concentrate on cultivating your own creativity!

4 THE EMPEROR

The Tarot is showing you a card which is the epitome of independence, of resisting external influences and of moving in your own totally self-determined direction. Up until now, although you haven't been happy about accepting orders from others, you have done so, feeling that one day you would be able to branch out in a totally independent direction, free from the external constraining influence of other people.

This may have ramifications on your work area, for example. You may have felt, over the last two years or so, that you could have done a lot better for yourself by starting up your own independent line of business than by continuing to serve those who were employing you.

On a relationship level, you may have felt limited, held back by the person that you are with, unable to get your life moving in the way that you felt it should have been.

Now is the time in which you can feel free to begin to tell these forces of limitation where to get off, so that you can live your life the way you feel it ought to be lived. This card is telling you to strike out!

The Emperor is about your own potential to say no to whatever you are unhappy with. It is he who breaks agreements in society about how things ought to be and challenges oppression. It is he who leads the revolutionary forces and suffers personally through his belief in the principles of equality, liberty and justice. But it is also he who, through his own excessive zeal for the cause in which he believes, can set in place of the preceding government a far worse dictatorship! In a society which has become so excessively centralized, with people feeling increasingly that they are unable to influence their destinies in any way whatsoever, it is the

Emperor type who tends to emerge, first as rebel, then as opposition, then as alternative, and finally as the new establishment. Many who in life start off wanting to change the political system end up as members of an establishment which may well have a different symbol on its headed notepaper, but which pursues the same policies as its predecessors.

But the Emperor is also about your own assertiveness; about not looking for others to take the place of your own potential for leadership. Because whenever we do this we are copping out of precisely those issues which we most need to take responsibility for.

What can you do to take more control over your own life?

5 THE HIEROPHANT

Around you there are many influences at work, only some of which may be apparent from your present perspective.

Now is the time for you to make whatever compromises are necessary in order to be able to continue in your present direction. In ancient times, the Hierophant was the master of ceremonies and thus was the original forerunner of the Masonic tradition, the spiritual tradition through which the ancient mysteries were handed down despite years of religious intolerance and persecution.

The basic meaning of this card is that now is a point in your life when you are ready to say to the world, 'Here I am' and the reply of the world will be, 'And here is the effect of all the causes, good, bad and indifferent, which you have made in the period leading up to now.'

The presence of this card is suggesting that your life has been a rather eccentric one – and probably always will be. But at this point you will increasingly see that even those who you have assumed to be very orthodox or conventional have actually led similar lives, beneath the surface level of immediately visible reality.

You are about to receive an initiation into the way in which the world works – remember, even in some of the trying experiences that lie ahead, that you are surrounded by friends and allies who, for reasons of their own, prefer to remain in the background ready to be of help if needed, rather than be so openly identified with your position.

The Hierophant was the 'Chairman' as it were of the Magical Order of the Golden Dawn, a semi-Masonic order set up around the end of the last century to enact symbolic journeys of its members through the doorways and pathways of the Tree of Life. The Hierophant would have to learn long speeches by heart which would then be recited in front of the new members; set-piece speeches in which he would go on about the significance of the cube, or Star of David, or the journey of the soul into the astral plane. He would pass on to the new member 'keys' of magical value – sometimes they would be angelic names, or things they could do to enhance their own magical powers in one way or another. Some of these spells would have to do with invisibility, or knowledge, or protection. So it was really a school that he was responsible for running. This school attracted many members of the intelligentsia, including a number of writers, historians and professors, as well as members of 'high' society, even as far up as the House of Lords. So, you can see that this card really has a lot to do with hierarchy, structure, traditions and so on. These days mystical knowledge is a lot more freely available than it was in the age when the church and its own form of orthodoxy had a much stronger grip over what got published and what was freely discussed in polite society. So, these days, the appeal of small esoteric societies has waned, as people are now able to get insight into their lives from a much wider range of spiritual practices than ever before.

Another aspect of the Hierophant is the relevance of initiation. In some societies around the world, the male members of the tribe have to go through some kind of initiation in which they are led out into the forest or desert for a certain period and left to face their own fears. The Hierophant is he who leads through the pathway of initiations such as these. They would always be regarded as symbolic turning-points for those concerned, and after being taken, there was no going back to the more juvenile states which preceded them. They always marked the divide between man and boy, woman and girl. In a sense, the ritual of marriage is an initiation in itself, in its original form, as it would originally mark the development of the married couple from childhood innocence to adulthood. In every religion, there are rituals to mark the symbolic passing of the soul through each of its major lifetime landmarks. The rite of a funeral is, in a sense, another example of this.

The Hierophant card touches upon all of these other areas as well.

6 THE LOVERS

This card has come up for you because it is talking about intensity in relationships that you are involved in with others. It is really saying that until now, your relationships have been pretty hit and miss as to whether they have worked out or not. Sometimes they have and sometimes they simply – and sadly – haven't.

Now you must begin to experience them from a new viewpoint, to realize that they are not just based upon affinity, but also upon communication and reality. In other words, you must see that your relationships depend not just upon feeling, but also upon how much you have in common with the other person and how well you are able to communicate with them too.

This card is saying that in any relationship scenario, be it love or friendship, you must regard any upsets as a challenge to be overcome and not just as a barrier.

Here we are also looking at the principle of duality in relationships. It may be that your partner is complementing certain aspects of your own personality – or challenging them.

This card is saying that instead of reacting to whatever is going on in your love life, just relax and experience it instead. Life's teachings come to each of us in many guises, sometimes in a very obvious form and sometimes in a less than obvious form. Here, the Tarot is saying, become aware of the fact that life's teachings are coming to you through the kinds of relationships which are forming around you. Learn from them.

But we are also looking at the principle of love in its wider sense. Whatever we love, we do well. In the realm of Tarot training, I know if someone is going to do well in their studies if they actually have a love of the Tarot. When this principle is at work in our lives, it is we who experience the fruits through both giving and receiving. For whatever – or whoever – we love, no time is too much to spend. We do not count. And thus we begin to tap into the universal spirit of giving which mystics have called God, or deity, or infinity. For those that have tasted of its essence, there can be no higher teaching than this.

What – or who – do you most love? What is it about your object of affection that draws you towards it in this way? Does your life feel empty without someone or something special which you can be involved with? Or are you able to create something to be at the centre of your life?

7 THE CHARIOT

In this card we see someone holding the reins of power in their hands and, we must suppose, the principle of strong leadership is being shown. But if we look in a little more detail, we can see that the reins of power which this man holds onto so determinedly are in fact connected to the two horses which drive his chariot.

The fact is that although you may well feel empowered under this influence, remember that to a greater extent than you realize, your position depends upon the continued good will and co-operation of other people who are also involved in the situation with you.

At the base of the chariot are two sphinxes, one white and the other black. They are saying that you will achieve balance here in your life by maintaining a sense of forward motion, not by staying passive, waiting for something to happen.

At this point, great power is being given to you, possibly from a higher spiritual plane of being. You must use this extra energy by doing something with it – other people are waiting for you to take the initiative. You must now create a game plan and mobilize the human resources which are now available to you. If you don't, rest assured that others will, and you will have missed an important chance. The Chariot is about the completion of projects, as well as their initiation. The wheels of the chariot invariably have to turn full circle if any sense of forward motion is to occur.

It is telling you to look around in your life and see what needs to be completed. You may be reminded of promises you have made which you have since forgotten about. When the Chariot card comes up in a spread it hints that now is an ideal period to fulfil commitments. It also touches upon the danger of entering into commitments from which it is difficult to withdraw. After all, in order to draw a chariot forward, you need horses, and you can't easily change these in midstream, can you?

The Chariot, because of its link with the astrological sign of Cancer, also touches upon the principle of our defences, because just as a crab protects itself wherever it goes by carrying its shell on its back, so in this card we are looking at the defences which we each of us employ for our own self-protection. What are your defences? In what way do you hide behind them? Do you still need all of them, or can some of them be thrown away?

Great power is given under this placing. The Strength card has come up for you and is saying that through the conflicts which you have had with your own weaknesses, you have gained some degree of mastery over others. And vice versa: that through the conflicts you have had with others, you now stand much more in control of yourself, of your own energies, and are more single-minded.

This card was traditionally represented in old Tarot decks as showing the battle between Hercules and the Nemean Lion. In more recent decks, the same principle has been shown by the image of a beautiful woman, serenely opening and closing the mouth of a roaring lion. The symbols are different in that in the former it shows the domination of one power by another, while in the latter it shows the transcendent influence of reason over passion.

This latter image is more in keeping with what the Tarot is trying to say to you. It is saying that it is by keeping your cool that you will be able to come out in top of whatever situation of conflict you are going through, or are about to go through.

Remember that the strongest weapon you have at your command at this time is the fact that you are not to rise to the bait of whatever provocation is made towards you.

Above the head of the woman in this picture, we see a figure of eight on its side, the symbol of infinity, which means that no matter what is occurring on the outer level of action in your life at this time, it too will change and move on to become something else.

Remember, just as the serenity of the woman is more powerful than the lion, so your own spirituality is a stronger force than the animalistic passions of yourself and also of others.

This card is calling upon us to examine where our real strength lies. We are so often used to thinking of ourselves as 'strong', especially when in perfect bodily health. But are we? All it takes for us to be reduced to whimpering wrecks is to step on a nail and get an infection. Or to develop a soar throat. Many people get very angry when a loved one is sick or ailing, basically because it is a reminder of their own frailty.

What are you doing with your own strength? Are you using it positively or are you wasting it on irrelevant jousting tournaments, left, right and centre? What are you doing that is helping others get in touch with their own strength?

9 THE HERMIT

In this card we can see that you have led something of a solitary life, always holding yourself back from other people, seemingly letting them into your life but not really doing so. This card suggests that you are a very private person, or have been up until now.

Your path has led you through some very solitary experiences and, symbolically, has been akin to a path that has run through a mountain range. Now you stand at the top of this same mountain and you hold a lantern outstretched in front of you.

You are just finishing a period of relative isolation, in which psychologically you have gone through a slimming process. Unnecessary layers of personality have been sheared away and you are probably feeling slightly worse for wear.

Now, this card is telling you, you must begin to think much more in terms of how you are going to find your way back down the mountainside, to the valley below where the rest of us live.

Your presence is required here, in the real world, where the rest of us can enjoy your company and get the benefit of your wisdom, of your experiences, no matter how isolated from us they may make you seem or feel. This is your next step.

The Hermit also touches upon the value of just going off by ourselves every now and again, just to clear our own minds. Some people find that they get real benefit from going to a monastery or ashram, for a period. Others are content just to go for walks in the park, alongside a river or to an ancient site such as Glastonbury Tor. If people aren't able to get away by themselves every now and again, they will resort to other, less positive ways of 'escaping' from the mental proximity of others, such as drugs and drink. The Hermit teaches us the need we each of us have to 'vanish' and the value in terms of heightened insight which we can derive from the experience.

Are you getting away enough, the Hermit is asking you? Are you making some time for yourself, forsaking all others? How else do you expect to hear that still small voice of the Higher Self through all of that din and racket that you call social life?

10 THE WHEEL OF FORTUNE

On the great Wheel of Fortune we see the sum total of life and death, with all the ups and downs of life, short-term and long-term.

Here, we are looking at the principle of expansion, of things growing and taking off right before our eyes! But without some element of control or direction things can get out of hand. After all, if everything in the garden is growing, then so are the weeds as well! And if you didn't do any pruning, you wouldn't even be able to get into the garden after a while, either! So, just as this card is talking about growth and abundance, recognize that there is a potential negative aspect even to this. A prescriptive measure, in looking at this card, is to recognize that it is important that we ascertain exactly what are the things that we want to see grow and develop, both in our own personal lives and in the society in which we live. There is certainly the need for some element of discrimination.

You are going through a period of increase, of abundance. This will have an effect of increasing whatever it is that you value. If your own values are purely on the material level, the set of influences which you are going through will make you very wealthy. If it is land that you are intent on buying, for example, then this card will enable you to grow and to prosper in that direction. If your values are also on the spiritual level, then this card will give you a sense of abundance here also.

Positive people will be entering into your life at this time. You will benefit from their contact and they will from you also. You may even be meeting people who are rich or even famous at this time. But don't fall into the trap of associating with people just because they are well-known or well-to-do or because they can provide specific help in your career: you would actually be missing the main reason for life having brought you into contact with them in the first place.

The best way of utilizing this experience is to learn from these people. That will require some element of humility on your part to be able to so do.

It is important to avoid excessive pride under this influence. You could well misrepresent yourself to others as being wilful, or too puffy or proud. If so, it would be a shame, because you may well tend to cut yourself off from valuable sources of support which would come in useful at a later point.

Some of what you consider to be important discoveries at this time may well represent a milestone in your own development. But others may well have already learnt for themselves these same things.

What are the things which you would like to see more abundantly available in your own life? What sort of things would you like to see growing more abundantly in society?

---

11 JUSTICE

Here in this card what we are seeing is a major balancing out of different aspects of your past, present and future taking place. At this time in your life, it is possible for you to restructure your life without any major crisis taking place as a result. This card is saying that you should not necessarily be on a continual clean-up and improvement campaign, especially in the area of your relationships. Instead, concentrate on the issues which are actively troubling the relationship: the rest you can safely afford to bypass for the time being.

In this card we are looking at the law of karma – the law of cause and effect. This card is saying that in accordance with the seeds which you have sown, you will begin to reap the harvest: what will be relevant will be those things which you have thought, said or done.

Therefore, look at how you can now influence the present situation while taking on board more responsibility, not less. You already have knowledge – you will find that you will come to exercise control by taking responsibility for what is going on around you. The way up for you is by moving in this direction: the way down is for you to run away, to retreat and to say to others, 'Look at what was done to me': don't allow yourself to become a victim. You may find it helpful to sit down and write up all the negative acts of commission and omission which you have perpetrated: against yourself, against the opposite sex, against your family, against your deepest principles, etc. It is only by reviewing your own weak spots or 'blind spots', that you will become sufficiently aware to be able to avoid repeating them.

·12 THE HANGED MAN

This card is looking at the principle of sacrifice at work in your life and it is saying that at the moment, you probably feel that people are making quite heavy demands upon your time, energy and money.

Sometimes in our lives, we are called upon by fortune to give unselfishly to a particular cause, to friends, to relatives, to something which we believe in or are a part of. This is one such point in your life. Someone in your circle of activity is asking a particular favour of you, and it may well be your immediate reaction to say, 'Well, what have you done to deserve such a favour?' The answer would be, of course, that in all probability the other person would have done nothing – or at least very little.

The presence of this card in your reading is suggesting that you shouldn't be too calculating in terms of whether the things which are now being asked of you have been earned.

At some earlier point in your life, you also were given support and help, and didn't thank the person who had helped you. You weren't expected to do so. Now, the time has come for you to do the same for someone else. At this point, show a sense of magnanimity, of generosity, of being big as a personality: in this way, you will win the favour of the Gods and earn for yourself an even greater blessing in the future.

It may well seem that events have almost literally stopped taking place in your life; that you have arrived at a standstill. Enjoy this period of suspension. Because generally, when events seem to have stopped happening in the plane of action, it means that the whole experience is changing gear and that things are therefore happening on an even deeper level of reality. Another aspect of this card is that it can tend to show someone looking at the world upside down. Could that be you? In what way?

13 DEATH

This is the card which even those people who are not familiar with Tarot symbolism are often able to recall, maybe from having seen a Hammer horror film on television. It shows Azrael, the Archangel of Death, descending upon ancient Egypt in response to the invocation of Moses. In this legend, Moses had asked for his people to be allowed to go free out of ancient Egypt, and when his requests had been repeatedly refused by the Pharaoh, he summoned the Angel of Death to come and take the firstborn of each Egyptian household.

This card, then, may be warning us about becoming too inflexible with regard to some of the changes which life sometimes makes upon us. It is simply saying that we must be flexible and not allow ourselves to get drawn into 'winner-takes-all' scenarios from which we stand to lose more than we could possibly gain.

This card is saying to you that a major period of change is taking place in your life – but that it is going to be extremely advantageous to you in the long run.

You may not feel that the time is right for you to have to make such major changes, but this card is really reassuring you and saying that what is being presented to you is an exceptional opportunity for you to get out of your rut and start to experience something different from anything that has gone on before now.

What are the umbilical cords which still link you to past patterns? What is stopping you from cutting them?

--------------------- 14 TEMPERANCE ---------------------

This card is showing an angel standing by a pool of water, pouring water from one cup to another. It shows the movement of the life force from one vessel or body into another. Water, the symbol of life itself from time immemorial, moves from the state of solid, when it is ice, through to liquid, and then from liquid to the state of air, when it evaporates. After a period spent in that form, it condenses, when it comes back down to earth in the form of rain, i.e. the downward motion of water in the card. So, we have a guided tour in this card through each of the elements, but with the essential and eternal quality of the life force remaining absolutely constant.

This card is inviting you to recognize the eternal and unchanging aspect of your own spiritual condition, that although you go through the experience of seeing constant change around you, you yourself as a spiritual creature are not whatever body you find yourself contained within in this lifetime.

This card is saying that at this point in life we have genuinely experienced a sense of spiritual and personal growth. Now we can begin to look back into our past with an awareness unfettered by the blinkers of ordinary consciousness and see what has really happened there to make us – or at least influence us – become the things which we are in the present.

It is a card which suggests great good fortune, if we take advantage of the present to look more closely at the decisions about ourselves which have led us to this present vantage point.

It is a period of considerable clarity, enabling us to define more clearly those things which we want to be, to do, and to have in the next cycle of activity as well.

This card is saying that it is by looking at our past from this perspective that we will more accurately be able to understand our present. At that point, it will be increasingly easy to determine our life direction, and to begin to move ahead to our goals and objectives.

The angel, or, more correctly, archangel which is shown here is Raphael, traditionally associated in ancient texts with healing. Thus the card is suggesting some kind of a healing process which is taking place in your life or which perhaps needs to take place. This card comes up a lot for people that have been involved in counselling, either giving counsel to others or receiving it themselves. Behind Raphael we see a road running into the distance, suggesting the past experiences which we have gone through, which have led us to where we are now. If you look carefully you will see the angel stands with one foot on land and the other on water. This represents the time when we emerged from the waters onto land, and thus became air-breathing creatures with lungs instead of gills. Thus we see from the posture of the angel that this card is all about the important evolutionary steps which we have as yet to make. What is there in your past that you could actively bring forward into present time to help you move forward? What is there in your life which still needs to go through the healing process?

Here we have the Tarot saying to you that there is some kind of energy blockage taking place. Quite probably you are suppressing your emotions and forcing your emotional response on the basis of a personality imprint made upon you at an earlier point in your life. You must 'unlearn' away from this pattern. You must get away from all the sources of negativity and annoyance which vex your soul and trouble your mind at this time. It is not necessary to overload your mind at the expense of your own sense of peace and harmony.

The Devil card often appears in a person's life when a challenge is being made against them. This challenge may come through other people – here, you must be strong enough to withstand the opposing forces representing the influence of these people: they may well be hidden or out of sight, not wanting to display themselves openly, preferring to work against you in a more surreptitious manner.

The basic message of this card stays the same, whether your opponents are fighting you openly or not: what you must do is stand by your principles, your ethics, and refuse to compromise with the forces against you.

Another aspect of the Devil is that it touches upon all of that which we feel we cannot give up or relinquish: all of our stuff, habits and routines, which we know aren't doing us any good at all, and which may in fact be holding us back from going ahead into what our futures may hold for us. What is it that you aren't prepared to say goodbye to?

Some people need devils, so that they can have an excuse for failure. 'Well, I tried to do X, but, well, it didn't work out, so it must mean it's not "intended" to work out.' Or they dramatize others in the role of the Queen or King of Darkness, against which they seem to lose their power of control. How can we rid our lives of casting others into this role? How can we come to see those who challenge us in life less as devils and more as our own personal trainers, leading us on to greater levels of self-empowerment?

16 THE TOWER

In this card we see a great tower being tested by the forces of nature. It represents everything that you have built up being put to the test.

From the financial standpoint, now is most definitely a time for you to conserve resources, almost fanatically. Any kind of excess would work against you under this set of influences.

It is vital that you use this period to clear as many debts as possible, karmic as well as financial. It may seem as though people in your life whom you had automatically assumed to be reliable are now proving themselves not to be.

You must immediately bypass normal habits and routines, and take control over whatever area of your life has started disfunctioning. Then, handling the situation and removing any danger in it, proceed to reorganize the relevant activity so that the situation is not constantly happening again and again.

Now is the time for you to apply your ethics – whatever they may happen to be – and that means examining that area of your life that is going wrong at this time and deciding what is best for you – and the society in which you live – on the basis of the greatest good for the greatest number.

Don't operate from a purely selfish dynamic – remember that others are relying on you for your qualities of leadership to help them get out of this mess as well!

What could you be doing in your life at this time that will come to be the foundation of something really positive in the future? What pattern should you be stopping here in the present, i.e. specifically not doing, which will enable you to avoid suffering at some future time period?

---

17 THE STAR

The Star card in your reading is showing you that after the storm there is a peaceful period in which you can now begin to go about making the kinds of changes to your life which recent pressures and tensions have led to.

This card is something of a healing influence, suggesting that you have been given a fair amount of teaching recently, and that the spiritual powers that be are now looking down on you and deciding to give you a break. Take advantage of this opportunity to learn about yourself and determine where you feel your long-term direction lies.

It has been said of this card that it shows a 'cooling off or a cooling down' period in a person's life, and there is something in this.

It is as though your life is 'in between acts', and you now have the chance to move out of the role of actor or spectator.

Nothing is expected of you. Under this set of influences, you are not going to have to be anything which you are not, or even to feel obliged to do anything in particular. It will bring good fortune for you to become more involved in humanitarian ventures.

By working in activities designed to help others, you will find your own path opening up.

Social-service ventures, working with the underprivileged, or those that have been through emotional trauma, alcoholism or drug addiction, could well be some areas of action which this card is suggesting you take a look at. How could you be of greater service to others less fortunate? How does it make you feel when you have really helped someone? Would you like to experience that feeling more often? What sorts of things might come to you from out of the blue if you did more along those lines?

------------------------------ 18 THE MOON ------------------------------

The Moon card here in your spread is showing that a very important gateway is being flung open for you: on either side of this gateway stand the Gods of Light and Darkness. You are warned to tread carefully here, fellow traveller!

Straight is the path and narrow is the way ahead for you on this path. Be not deceived by those around you that are appealing to your emotions, against your better judgement. You must most certainly be ruled by your reason; keep your feet on the ground and try not to be so strongly influenced by your emotion or imagination.

Trust only a portion of what you can see and none of what others are suggesting to you.

It is a difficult period for you to know your friends and to be able to distinguish between those that are genuinely on your side and those who are merely fair-weather friends.

It is not a time for giving up your own personal responsibility. It would be good for you to withdraw from the dark, shady things in which you may well be involved, before your fingers get burned. Look at it this way: if you aren't sure whether an involvement with someone or something is positive or negative, ask yourself, 'What good can come from this?' and then ask yourself the question, 'What bad can come from this?' In asking yourself these questions, you will immediately find your answer and then it will be down to you to be guided by that.

The spiritual light which you think is burning so brightly at this time could well be misleading you, allowing you to see reflected in the world an illusion of your own hopes and fantasies.

Another aspect of the Moon is that it does represent our dreams, our fantasies, our illusions. And our dreams are there to instruct us, to help us learn about ourselves. What could you be doing to help yourself realize your dreams in a practical way?

The Moon also signifies the yearning for fulfilment. What is it that you would like to experience in your life which is eluding you at the moment?

The Moon is also a traditional symbol of mother, because it brings into being all of the latent aspects of creation in the universe into manifestation. If you are a woman, it might be asking you about how you see your own role as a mother or as a mother at some point in the future. If you are a man, it might be asking you to take a look at your relationship with your own mother and/or your relationship with the mother(s) of your own children. How do you feel about all of this?

19 THE SUN

XIX — THE SUN

Here we see the emblem of true light, of warmth, and of growth and development taking place in all areas of your life.

Your physical health should be especially good under this influence, although you shouldn't do anything deliberately which will weaken this power.

Plans which you have had brewing for some time can come to fruition now and you are in a position to act decisively, knowing clearly from where your strength is derived and from where you can expect challenges.

It is a very positive period and wherever you go and whatever you do, people will follow you in your actions and come to support you.

It is an excellent period for you to travel or to make connections with people from substantially different backgrounds from yourself, people whose ideas about life you will find refreshingly different from those of your own people.

Use this influence, therefore, to learn from them and to enjoy their company. Relationships formed under this influence need not be so short-lived as you seem to think they must inevitably be. They can in fact last a long time, if you want them to enough.

The Sun also represents the role of father. It could therefore be touching upon the relationship which you have had with your father. If you are a man, it might be getting you to look and see how you could be a good father, or an even better father, towards your own children. If you are a woman, it might be asking you to take a look at your relationship with your own father and/or with the father(s) of your own children. What are your feelings on this?

--- 20 JUDGEMENT ---

This card will come up for you when your life is on the brink of a major transformation. This transformation will bring into being a new relationship or deepen an old one. A new one which comes into being now will be notable for the strength of the feelings involved. It could hardly be described as casual. There is a compulsive quality about the energies that drive you and your partner together, but this is not at all negative.

It will merely seem to both of you as though this relationship was inevitable and you will both find that it is a learning process of the best possible kind. You will now discover that love is less conscious and that you act more from sheer compulsion than you had ever realized.

Here, you may well feel that you are playing out a scene still held over from a past life – and it is quite possible that you indeed are. You may well decide to throw everything over and change the country in which you have decided to settle.

The trick to handling this influence is in not allowing this experience to become destructive, but in drawing upon its energies to be uplifting, not enslaving.

The title of this card is interesting, because the scene of the traditional Day of Judgement is not taken just from the Bible, as most people seem to think. All of the world's religions believe in an ordeal which must be undertaken by every mortal soul that must be weighed in the balance of the Gods at the end of its earthly life. It is allowed into the afterlife only if it has successfully passed the test or tests which it must face. At this trial, the soul is invariably asked questions by each of the Gods – and Goddesses – in turn. Those souls which fail are invariably destroyed by a demon, or a great dog, or something similar. Those that pass the tests are taken off to enjoy the beautiful scented gardens, frequented by beautiful young people. Common to all of these widely different faiths, there is this universal scene of judgement. Even in Buddhism, there is great emphasis on the soul being rewarded for its good deeds and punished for its bad ones as well.

What this card may well be asking you is, 'Are you being too self judgemental?'

At this time you can reach a stable understanding of what you are, and you can take control of your life and prepare to achieve your goals in the world.

This is primarily a time of preparation and this card isn't saying that you will necessarily reach all of your goals now. It is looking more at the significance of the foundation. The actual building work will be up to you.

This card also suggests a period of review – in other words, looking back over your previous successes and actually giving yourself credit for what you have already attained. And less criticism for what you haven't attained – as yet.

The most central thing here is that you are able to attain an experiential grasp of the nature of the causes of things – not just an intellectual understanding. It also suggests the need to absorb or assimilate past experiences – even setbacks which have all played a part in the learning process up until this point.

This card suggests that areas such as your professional or business life will run smoothly at this time. The people with whom you come into contact will tend to appreciate your calm, controlled way of handling your work, and they can see and appreciate the results of your past experience.

Your outlook on life has reached a point of equilibrium. You have a good understanding of how you look at life and it works well enough that you may not question it very much.

The one danger is that you can tend to fall into the trap of thinking that you've got the whole thing sussed. Continue to re-examine your life and be open to suggestions made by others as to how specific things in your life might be improved.

Even if your life is satisfactory now, it may not always be. It never does any harm to have one or two tricks up your sleeve just in case you might need them in the future!

Another aspect of the World card is the existence of opportunities disguised. Disguised as problems? Possibly! But waiting to be discovered so that they can be turned around.

What needs to be turned around in your life? Do you sometimes carry the World on your shoulders? How could you experience the World more as your own personal oyster?

THE MINOR ARCANA

The Minor Arcana (Minor Mysteries) consists of 56 cards. These each show different everyday situations and archetypes, or personality types, at work in our lives. They indicate aspects connected with having, thinking, doing and being. Instead of thinking of them as Mysteries, it is probably more helpful to think of them as Explanations, indicating how we might each of us achieve more meaningful and more fulfilling lives.

First we have the suit of Coins, sometimes known as Pentacles, which represents the element Earth. It shows aspects of life to do with work, money, space and that which we own. It is therefore where much of our sense of security comes from.

The Suit of Coins

──────────────── THE ACE OF COINS ────────────────

In this card we are shown a doorway which is opening up for you in the area of work or in business opportunities. Before you stands a new path, stretching out towards the horizon, with a gate at the end. The doorway lies open for you to begin to make progress in your financial life.

But this card is showing more than that. Your present direction lies in terms of establishing mastery over the material conditions of life. This is your next step spiritually, also. The fact that you are now being brought face to face with some of the economic realities of life and are now being summoned to exercise command over them, does not mean that you are being diverted from your path: rather the reverse – now you are to apply the lessons you have learned previously.

Up until this point you may have experienced a sense of confusion about your true abilities and how you would be best advised to use them to further yourself in the world. Now if you take a good look you can begin to see more clearly in what direction you should be moving.

This card does not by itself guarantee that you will necessarily take advantage of this new set of opportunities – but it does say that you should.

Be stable, fixed, constant and persistent in your aims and purposes.

With this card you are shown standing with your back to a great ocean, juggling two completely different spheres of material action in your hands. Here the Tarot is reminding you that you are a juggler in the great game that is life and that you must be prepared to be flexible, mentally.

Life is calling upon your ability to be versatile, and that is going to involve you being able to bypass normal habits and routine ways of thinking that don't serve your interests in the present.

You may well be faced with the prospect of moving, either literally, as in the case of a job move, or domestically, such as in a house move.

You may, for instance, have become quite rigid in how you have lived your life up to this point and have possibly become quite content with the pattern which it has taken.

At the least, you have got into a groove which this card is now indicating you must begin to move out of and into new horizons.

The basic key-note here is flexibility. Change, under this set of influences, is a relatively harmonious process, and it is best to undertake whatever steps are required in order to realign your life with the new season of possibility that is opening up for you now.

If you resist the change process at this point, or fail to see the opportunity that is there waiting for you to respond, then you may successfully resist this stage, but the loss will be yours alone.

We are now seeing you in the role of apprentice: in the process of learning and developing new skills and abilities which will empower you to be able to make real progress in the world of action.

This card sees you wearing the hat of a student, but that need not necessarily be at any formal college or with any official training programme. Here we have an interpretation of this stage of your life as a learning stage. Positive people and positive influences are around you, which can help you in this process.

But there is the need to recognize that you don't know everything, or have access to all the facts in a particular matter. So there is the need to suspend judgement – you are still learning under this influence.

Be responsive to the lessons which these new people are bringing to you. Don't by any sense of pride lose the opportunity to take on board the new knowledge and skills which they are bringing in their wake. Or it may be that this new teaching may come from people you have known for some time, but who now are suddenly assuming this teaching function.

THE FOUR OF COINS

You certainly have got money matters on your mind at the moment! I am looking at you with your hands reaching out for extra money. There is a sense of urgency here, which may or may not have anything to do with the fact that there really is any genuine need, but which may have more to do with your own insecurity.

Money must be brought together here, because whether you need this money for something special or just for the sake of the extra peace of mind which you feel will come about through having it, the fact is that this is the direction in which your energy is flowing at this point in your life.

The philosophy of the Tarot is that only by first fulfilling your earthly desires will you become ready to transcend them.

Now you must go out and simply bring together whatever it is out there that you really need. Remember, money is an energy flow, it is a symbol of value. By strengthening yourself financially at this time, you will be readying yourself for the next stage on your life's path.

But ultimately, this card is also saying that you will have to develop a greater sense of being able to trust the universe around you and to realize that by opening your life to higher spiritual energies, you will find you heart's true desire.

THE FIVE OF COINS

At this point in your experience we see you walking down a long dark tunnel, alone and impoverished. There are others walking beside you on this small back road of your life. It is just at the moment that it merely *seems* that you are alone.

As we look at you through this card, we see you just about getting along in life, but you are moving ahead slowly, with your eyes fixed on the ground.

However difficult your path may seem at this time, remember that there are others around you who are also struggling along this same road. This could well be suggesting a time of self-questioning, but you must continue to move ahead despite all of your doubts. It may seem as though you can only move one step at a time: it doesn't matter – move ahead at this pace if this is the rate at which you can progress.

But lift your head up – don't get so immersed in the mundane details of life.

Remember that the whole of our lives are based on cause and effect – we will get out of our lives what we put into them. You may not be aware of what it is that you have done that has led to this period of difficulty, but the way out is for you to remember that this too will pass, and it will pass more quickly if you are able to reach out to those around you who are faring less well than you.

THE SIX OF COINS

What we are looking at here is the principle of sharing, of generosity. You are portrayed here in this card as being involved in a sharing process of some kind, probably financially.

In this card we see you standing at the centre of attention with a small group of people around you. These people may be known to you at this time and you may be aware that in them you have an audience. They are watching and waiting to see how you are going to distribute your energies and in what projects you are going to involve yourself over the coming period.

You are surrounded by competing demands, by different interests – all making claims upon your loyalty, suggesting that you owe primary allegiance to *them*.

At this point in your life you must decide to reward your supporters on the basis of the loyalty with which you have been treated.

It is not a time to be influenced by expediency, to be tempted into a course of action on the basis of temporary gain, but the real need is to reward friends and allies. And to reward each of them in accordance with the loyalty and support you have received from them in the past.

—————————————— THE SEVEN OF COINS ——————————————

Here we see someone who has been working in a particular field of activity for quite some time but who has yet to experience visible, tangible results to show that what they have been doing has been worthwhile.

You may well feel that some important project or some important part of your life has been absorbing a very considerable amount of energy and that you have as yet to see the full fruits of your labour, that you have yet to experience the harvest season of the crop that you have been working on so diligently over the last cycle of activity.

Quite possibly this project has been a creative one or at least one which has taxed your skills to an unprecedented degree.

This card is saying that you are now arriving at a point at which you will begin to experience this new harvest season. But keep going. Don't even think about jacking it all in and going off to start something else. Your mission at this time is to finish off, to complete all those things which you are still working on.

It is not a time to abandon your responsibilities, however tempting that might seem at this time. You would simply have to go through the same lessons all over again, at a different time and in a different place.

In this card I can see that on quite a deep level you are successfully applying the lessons of the past. You are shown as being extremely busy, and the natural outlet for your energy at this point is through embracing tasks and responsibilities. Whether you like it or not, others are now seeing in you someone who has successfully handled the lessons of life.

In you they see someone who is effective and who is able to show them how they may go about improving the quality of their own lives. It may even be that others are imitating you, consciously or otherwise. Let them do so, without any sense that they are going to challenge you, either personally or professionally.

Here you are represented as the craftsman at work. Notice that the craftsman holds in his hands the same tools as the apprentice who we saw in the Three of Coins. Don't be so deprecating of your own role. What you are involved in is part of something much greater.

There is historical significance in your daily efforts and this card is inviting you to share in this new perspective; you are symbolically a master builder, involved in the rebuilding of a new temple through which the higher powers may manifest themselves in a visible format.

The path you have moved along up until now has – to put it mildly – been an adventure. Not that every adventure is a success story by everyone's estimation, but your adventure is now working out more harmoniously and successfully that at any other time.

You are now at a point of achievement, either in the worldly sense or at least in the sense that the most important projects you started some time ago have begun to yield their full fruit.

You must allow yourself to enjoy the blessings which you have bestowed upon yourself. You must allow others to validate your abilities and to acknowledge you as someone who has these abilities and who has, and is, successfully using them.

This is a period in which you can safely and pleasantly enjoy the sense of achievement that is now open to you; go forward, therefore, secure in the knowledge that you have earned the benefits of the material world.

In a deep and karmic sense, you are now being paid for all the times for which you were never paid before.

Here we are looking at a sense of fruition and fertility in all aspects of life.

In your situation at this point, you are involved in joint finances and major investment decisions. The decisions which you are about to take in these areas will have a significant impact on your life over the next major time period. There is a real need to base your policies on tried and tested ground, not because there is any particular sense of confusion, but because it is important that the next period of activity should represent an outgrowth of the past, without any sudden departures from previous policies.

In particular, any decisions you take should not so much be made by you alone, but should be made in consultation with all the parties involved, especially partners. If you act in isolation at this point, you will find yourself in isolation later on.

———————— THE PAGE OF COINS ————————

This influence will present many opportunities for achievement. At this time you will be able to strengthen your life so that each area can withstand pressure later on. You will accomplish nothing at this point without very considerable effort on your part. You will be learning the lessons of care and responsibility.

Recognition, especially from people in positions of power over you, may come now. But you will have to do everything in your power to live up to their high expectations of you. This card is suggesting that you should have more patience and perseverance than is normally the case.

You are able to work in a disciplined and careful manner and make your work last longer, to be of a higher quality.

THE KNIGHT OF COINS

This influence can bring both fulfilment and difficulty. Some time back, you went through a period of extreme difficulty, but at the same time you were able to make new beginnings, which are now starting to pay off.

This is a time of tremendous responsibility and hard work, either to guarantee the successful conclusion of your old projects and activities or at least to cut your losses when they simply are not working out.

In those areas of your life that you have handled successfully; whether that is in your job, your home life, your love life or wherever, the responsibility of bringing your activities to a successful climax will be considerable and will certainly limit to some degree your freedom to do exactly as you please.

Don't take on any projects at this time that are not directly connected to whatever you are currently engaged in. The additional work-load would only serve to dissipate your energies – whereas what is required at this time is a focalizing of them.

This is a time of hard work, responsibility and continued perseverance.

At this time your relationships will work for you in very practical ways. You understand how you need to have others work with you and you are willing to compromise with others in order that the both of you can progress. At this point in your life, you are not too idealistic.

Professional, business and other relationships are taking place at the moment, occupying your attention. Both you and the people you are in association with expect a great deal from each other, and this card is saying that much can be attained.

This is a time of psychological and physical equilibrium. If you have been under par, in either body or mind, this influence will help tremendously with the healing process.

This is also a good time to examine your ideals and goals, for it is possible to actualize them in various ways now.

If you feel that there are things around you which need doing, then this card is saying get on with doing them. Now is not a time of just sitting around, waiting for something to happen.

Here you are likely to be feeling good, with enough confidence to handle just about anything. It is a period when you feel optimistic, as though you can do whatever you want. Actually, you may be somewhat overconfident, so be careful not to take on more than you can comfortably handle.

At this point, several time-consuming projects may be coming to a head at once. This could be either quite advantageous or difficult, depending on how well you have estimated your capacities in the past.

This may also be a time of restlessness, for you feel that your everyday world isn't big enough or doesn't provide enough experience for you. If you feel this way, you must go about enlarging the scope of your activity, but again, be careful not to overreach.

Be careful to avoid conflicts with people who stand out as authority figures – you may have to reassure them that in pursuing your aims and objectives, you are not posing a challenge or a threat towards them. In this way, you can win over to your side many people who would otherwise feel a bit wary about allowing you to pass by.

The Suit of Swords

The suit of Swords represents states of mind and also states of conflict. It shows how, with resolution, we may win through on life's battlefield. It represents the element Air.

────────────── THE ACE OF SWORDS ──────────────

In your hand stands a symbol of great power, the Ace of Swords. It is as if you have drawn Excalibur from the anvil. You have been hacking your way through a great jungle – the jungle of life – and now you stand poised on the verge of a great victory.

This battle may have just been fought or it may be something which you are just about to enter into. Whatever the situation, rest assured that no matter how much it may seem as though the balance of power is against you, in the strength of your own hands is the key to your achievement.

Remember that all of the great figures of history and of mythology have had to go through similar battles, and that although the Gods do not take away problems, they do strengthen those whom they wish to see succeed.

—————— THE TWO OF SWORDS ——————

Here we see you sitting with your back to the great ocean of life, with a long sword in each hand. Around your head and covering your eyes is a blindfold, preventing you from being able to see the consequences of the very important decisions with which you are faced.

The Tarot is telling you that although you are feeling very much at the crossroads, it is probably best that you try to postpone making any important resolutions or decisions. The situation is just too confusing. There are too many variables involved and there is too much at stake for you to be able to move ahead.

If you take any action impulsively, you could easily slide further and further into the mire of confusion.

THE THREE OF SWORDS

We are looking at a heart which has been pierced by three swords, and which bleeds openly. Here we have one of the great symbols of heartbreak, relevant either for the present, or a warning that perhaps a past experience of heartbreak is in danger of repeating itself, *unless* you can very quickly learn to communicate better with the people in your life whom you love.

There is the potential here for terrific misunderstanding – only you can save the day for all concerned by getting out of your present attitude of nonchalance and making sure that those around you actually understand what you are trying to do.

It is a time for you to be more up front about actually telling people what you want from them, what your own needs are. You can take this a step further and ask them what their needs might be. It is possible that you think you already know. This card is warning you to think otherwise. At some point in your past you experienced heartbreak. This happened basically because you didn't know about communication and how powerful a remedial tool it can be. A tool is only as powerful as the amount of use it is given. Communication is such a tool. Use it!

THE FOUR OF SWORDS

The Four of Swords here is indicating that although your situation has been extremely tense up until now, there is now a releasing of tension and anxiety from within you. Don't hold on to the tensions of the past – now is your opportunity to put all of this behind you and learn to relax a little. You simply can't go on fighting yesterday's battles.

Now is a period of rest, in anticipation of some of the battles which tomorrow may bring.

This card is also showing that this is the time to take that much-desired vacation or to start up that recreational activity which you have put off until now, due to various pressures.

It is also a time in which you can look around and discover new ways to begin to achieve release. There is a sense of boredom in this card, in that some of the things which you used to find fun may now appear stale and humdrum. Well, in a way this is a good sign, because it means that you are growing and therefore changing. Time to move on and find new things to help you to unwind!

THE FIVE OF SWORDS

What may seem slightly gloomy about this scenario is that swords have been crossed and a parting of the ways seems about to take place as a direct result. It may seem at first glance as though an important relationship has broken up for you, possibly as a result of someone else's interference or as a result of your own lack of care and attention. But to look at your situation from this point of view would be to fail to understand the true significance of what is going on.

The sense of separation which is there in your life is telling you that we are all hitch-hikers through time and space, and that we come together for different reasons and that we part from each other when our lives' paths move in different directions.

Not much can be done to amend whatever damage has been done – now is the time to pack your emotional suitcases and move on further down the road of life. Rest assured that as you continue to grow emotionally, upsets like this will not affect you as much as they are at this time. The first 20 times are always the worst!

We see you here being ferried on a small boat from one coastline to another: in other words, making a transition in your life from one style of existence to another, quite different, quite distinct. There is the sense of defeat here – you feel that in some way the forces of life have conspired together to bring about your reversal.

There is no defeat here, only the need for you to retreat and reach higher ground, so that you can regroup your forces to bring about the great victory which this card promises.

At this point, though, don't lose heart or your sense of mission. Before each momentous accomplishment there is always a moment in which a moment of self questioning occurs. There are times in all of our lives when we have to pull back, or even pull out completely. Life is not always a never-ending series of unlimited successes; there are always setbacks or times in which we feel with hindsight that maybe we could have done more.

Be more on your guard and be less trusting of the people that you have delegated to. Here you must take much more direct control and basically become less reliant upon others to do things for you.

There may well be the need to make your home more secure against danger from fire or theft. It wouldn't be a bad time to save up some money, either.

It is a time in which a little bit more time and effort must be put into some simple precautionary measures which may well turn out to be totally unnecessary, but which could conceivably come in useful.

Health-wise, have you thought about taking vitamins? Or having a checkup? In your love life, do you practise safe sex? In your home, why not secure the windows, fix stronger locks or have that burglar alarm fitted? Have you checked your bank statements to ensure that monies are accurately recorded going in and being paid out?

It seems as though you can't get out of your present situation and you can't stay in it either. Tremendous frustration is shown here in this card: not only are you blindfolded and unable to make decisions on a sure footing at the moment, but you are surrounded by a small forest of swords, hemming you in and making progress out of existing limitation impossible.

You must bide your time. Remember that the time for you to act will come, and will come shortly.

All you can do at the moment is to exercise patience. Any movement to get out of the existing situation will only result in further pain and loss. The test is of your patience. Not an easy one at all: any action will be better than none at all.

—————————— THE NINE OF SWORDS ——————————

You and you alone can act to set yourself free from all of those negative influences of the past; from all of those ties that bind you to the sources of suffering. You are feeling very cut off from other people, very separate, as though no one can see through to the real you underneath the surface you are outwardly presenting.

The pain and sorrow of the past will not fade away instantly, but it *will* fade away. What you can do now is begin to open up and let the sun in.

For this to happen, you must begin to dig all of the loneliness out of your present and communicate your feelings to others.

You must begin to open up if you want other people to begin to see the real you – don't stay out there in isolation! You may well have to look around and discover new channels in which you can begin to relate effectively to those around you. You alone can do this work. It can either take a long time or it can take a very surprisingly short period of time. Which are you going to let it be? Come on, get cracking and dig your way out!

THE TEN OF SWORDS

Major changes are now taking place and it may well seem as though vast sections of your life are being swept away. Certainly you are going through a process of major psychological change and discovery.

The more you hang on to any rigid notion of who you are and how you should be treated, the more difficult you will find this period.

At major stages of life, a snake will shed its skin. You must begin to shed the psychological skin you have worn for so long now and although this is going to be difficult, this is precisely what you must do.

It may well seem as though there is no one around to help you during this crisis. You must move through this painful period of metamorphosis with the confidence that you will shortly be transforming from a caterpillar into a magnificent butterfly. While this change process is going on, you will feel that you are losing your landmarks, the reference points which we each have and which we all need to give us a sense of stability and security. When we lose our landmarks, we become quite unsettled and confused. We feel that any sense of continuity is gone when this happens, which is one of the reasons why we feel so sad and depressed when someone dies. But let us be of good cheer, because nothing is achieved without a sacrifice of some sort. Sacrifice means the rendering up of something of lesser value in exchange for something of much greater value. In order to make omelettes, we must first of all break eggs and then discard the shells. We don't mourn the loss of the eggshell when we sit down and eat the eggs, do we? So, likewise, ultimately there is no loss, only a change in what we see and can experience.

THE PAGE OF SWORDS

This card suggests that you have a strong need to assert yourself, but you may do it in a way that provokes conflict with others. On the other hand, this could possibly be a time of very vigorous and successful work, in which you will succeed by asserting your own individuality towards others in some way.

Be very careful about feeling jealous and resentful about someone else's success. You may feel that their success was stolen from you, but that is not true. Work for your own interests, not against someone else's.

You may encounter serious opposition from others. The best way for you to deal with this is to encounter the other person in the open and get it over with. Otherwise, you will have to deal with your own or the other person's sullen irritability. If you have a vague, undefined anger at the world in general, it is because you have tried to ignore the anger or hurt within yourself. Now it is bubbling up in a form so disguised that you cannot so easily diagnose its source.

This card has come up in your reading to tell you that you should avoid rash and impulsive actions, for they will alienate others, create enemies and, in the long run, undermine your own interests. Your ego energies run rather high, but in such a way that you are likely to assert yourself inappropriately. You may feel that you can conquer the world and, therefore, issue completely inappropriate challenges to the people around you. Most frequently you are expressing these feelings as irritability, excessive impatience and general touchiness.

On the other hand you may have to contend with someone else who is acting in this way. In this case there is nothing to do but be as patient as possible, fighting back only if there is a serious issue at stake. Remember that under this card you will have a strong tendency to regard all issues as serious as if they involve your pride.

This is a good time for getting work done, if you can control your impulsive behaviour. Any task that requires sheer physical energy with little finesse or attention to detail would be excellent, because it would allow you to work off energy without totally suppressing the natural impulsiveness that you are going through.

THE QUEEN OF SWORDS

In this card you are feeling extremely restless and impatient with your daily routine and inclined to seek out new experiences and activities. This impulse is not so uncontrollable that it will seriously disrupt your life, but you will be driven to make a number of changes in your daily routine that introduce some new excitement.

Your thinking under this card is more impulsive and changeable than usual. On the one hand, this will make you rather unpredictable and fickle, but it also gives you the capacity to break out of the rut, both psychologically and physically.

More to the point, you will be able to make practical use of your new insights in everyday life.

In your drive for new experiences, you may well be seeking out new friendships or associate with more exciting and stimulating friends.

You will not be particularly patient with restrictions, nor will you be very disciplined about your work. In fact you will tend more to the erratic, valuing your own independence over discipline and order.

This is an excellent time to make moves towards realizing important goals in your life. But you will have to make some changes in the course of action that you originally planned. Don't worry – your new plans will undoubtedly be an improvement on the old ones. You will work zealously towards your goals now and you should have enough energy to carry you through against any opposition which you might encounter.

This is also a good time for group goals and objectives.

You may have to strive very hard to get anywhere, but, in so doing, your goals when you reach them will be far more permanent and far reaching. If you are unclear about what you are doing in some area, this will be a very good time to look inside yourself to find out what you really want to do. You should not and cannot move until you are absolutely clear about your objectives. A considerable change in your self-understanding may be one of the benefits to derive from this influence.

If you do understand yourself and have a clear picture of what you want to achieve, then proceed full steam ahead and do not worry. Just avoid stepping on other people's toes unnecessarily.

The Suit of Wands

The suit of Wands (or rods, as it is sometimes known) represents the element Fire, and shows energy, action and power. It indicates independent initiative.

──────────────── THE ACE OF WANDS ────────────────

Now is a period in which you feel empowered, strong and able to get into motion the projects you have dreamed of doing for so long. We are looking at a wand or staff being presented to you, appearing almost magically out of thin air and materializing in front of you.

It is the time to act decisively to grasp the full measure of the opportunities before you.

Don't be put off by other people's seeming apathy – you are the master of the present situation, as long as you do go ahead and take the full initiative opening up for you. Dare to struggle, dare to win. It is all down to your own individual resourcefulness. Don't wait around wondering what other people are going to do. In one sense, you are already waiting at the finishing line for some other runner to come along! Get moving on past this line and then you will have truly succeeded in winning the race. Be assured that there are other contenders in this 'race', even if you can't see them. You may have had an exceptionally good idea, or even have invented something. This card is saying that you must now move ahead very quickly indeed to get it patented, or in the hands of a publisher, or at least moving so that *you* can be the one to get the recognition for it. It is strange, but whenever someone thinks of a really good idea, someone else has thought of it as well. Look at the time the light bulb was invented. Simultaneously across the world about half a dozen other people thought of it. Thomas Edison was the guy who got all the fame and glory, because he was the first one to get it patented and in his name. This phenomenon has been given many names – morphic resonance, the 'hundredth monkey effect', to name but two.

THE TWO OF WANDS

People around are giving you advice for virtually all aspects of life, attempting to influence you, out of a desire to get you on what they each perceive as the 'right track'.

But few – if any – of them are aware of where you are coming from and of what your true needs are in your current situation. Thus the influence they bring to bear may be misleading or, at best, simply irrelevant.

On a slightly deeper level, though, the influence you are going through is bringing some kind of deep teaching into your life, possibly through someone you have known for years. They themselves may not even be aware of the powerful set of lessons which are flowing through them into your life. Or, it may be that you now find yourself in the role of counsellor, with many people coming to you for advice and information.

You are being portrayed by the Tarot as standing on a symbolic borderline, just about to make the transition from one country, as it were, to another.

Now your powers of leadership are to be demonstrated and the people around will be watching to see how far you are going to put into practice your beautiful philosophic ideals.

Your sincerity of purpose is to be shown to a wide audience, but you yourself will not be aware of the identity of that audience. And neither should you even let on that you know they are watching. Just get busy with all of the plans you have been nurturing for so long.

A massive gateway is opening: a doorway into a group activity or venture in which the central test at this time is whether you are able to sacrifice your own interests as an individual to serve the interests of your group as a whole.

The basic principle here is one of teamwork. You must come at this time to recognize that no one ever gets to make it solely by their own efforts but, to a lesser or greater extent, through acting in co-operation with one's group or team, whatever that particular group or team may be at this time.

For a group to function effectively, each member must make certain sacrifices for the benefit of the team as a whole.

This card is telling you to ask not so much what your team can do for you, but rather what you can do for your team.

THE FIVE OF WANDS

The situation you are enmeshed in at this point is one of considerable conflict, partly between you and others, but even more fundamentally between you and yourself.

This card is saying that all forms of discord that are manifesting in your world of action are the direct result of inner conflict, cross-purposes and false intentions.

To reconcile the outer world, you must first take responsibility for allowing the present battle to have taken place. With regard to your opponents in the outer world, push through the barriers which these represent with an absolutely fierce determination. Take no prisoners, for now is the time for complete ruthlessness: not in the sense of deliberately causing harm to others for no reason, but rather in the sense of consciously determining where your long-term interests are.

You must now be bolder than you would normally give yourself credit for!

THE SIX OF WANDS

The Six of Wands shows you riding a great white horse as leader of a victory procession into a captured city.

The forces of opposition which have held out against you are no longer able to withstand your power. There is barely any reason to continue a full-scale attack on whatever and wherever this opponent may be.

Rather, now is the time for you to marshal your forces, be they money, human resources, time, energy, and so on, into a major plan to rebuild those aspects of your life which require your attention. You will certainly be expected by others to respond to their needs in ways which are markedly different to treatment they may have received up until now.

It may be a mistake to play into their hands by reacting in an over-predictable style.

Better still, this card is suggesting that you keep your competitors guessing a little, by making a few sideways moves instead of the obvious direct thrust which you are now impatient to make.

—————————— THE SEVEN OF WANDS ——————————

The balance of forces against you at this time is very considerable. This card shows you fighting with one big staff or club against a whole host of smaller, but more numerous clubs.

The entirely wrong way out of this impasse is for you to rise to the bait and attempt to take on all of the opposing forces in one fell swoop. For you to even begin to attempt this would result in your being decimated at the first move. But standing by and doing nothing would be equally unacceptable. You simply cannot watch that which you have worked so consistently for being negated or reduced by the actions of others at this time. You cannot stand by and do nothing.

How then, can you resolve this dilemma? The answer here is that you must initially step back out of this battleground and then work out a plan to eliminate each of the opposing forces one by one, instead of trying to do so all at once.

This will require patience, but it is not the fundamental test here – the fundamental test is that of strategy.

—————————— THE EIGHT OF WANDS ——————————

All of a sudden it seems as though your life has taken off. Now, instead of wondering in which direction you should begin to move in order to develop your life potential, you are faced with a startling array of different projects, of different possibilities, all leading off to totally new places.

You will certainly find this amazing variety of potential directions quite disorienting, unless you can consciously sit down and recall precisely what original objectives or priorities have led you to this point.

What exactly were those things that you wished to be, to do, to have, that so inspired you to undertake all of these actions? What were those things that you felt you were not, that you could not do, or which you could not have, that stand out in such contrasting colours to where you are now?

Now is the time for you to get moving with that study or journey for which you have waited so long.

Motion is the keyword of this particular influence. But if you sit back and do nothing, the resulting benefit of this positive time period will almost certainly be zero. Move!

—————————— THE NINE OF WANDS ——————————

You are being described in this card as someone who has received a setback or whose interests haven't been advanced in the way that they should have been.

Not that there has been any element of betrayal at work here, but through neglect or incorrect delegation of duties and responsibilities to unqualified people, there has been a sense of loss.

You stand in a circle of staves at this time, nursing your wounds, drawing upon the lessons of the recent past in order to more adequately prepare yourself for the next cycle of action and advancement.

Don't, though, fall into any negative mental pattern of doubt or distrust of your fellow human beings. This is the fundamental test of this influence.

The way through is to consciously develop a *greater* sense of the basic goodness of your fellow human being, not less.

Around you stand many people, all of whom wish to add something of their own to your present situation to relieve your plight, to make your path smoother.

Allow them to come into your life a little more than you are doing at the moment – they wish to become your allies: let them. By allowing people to help you, you truly help them. Even if you feel you can do everything by your own efforts at this time, this card is saying that you should be a bit more prepared to accept support from others.

You are shown in this card staggering along under an extremely heavy burden, either in terms of your workload or in terms of the extent to which you unconsciously allow others to place their burdens upon your shoulders.

The load is heavy and it is becoming heavier: there is almost a cumulative effect in the way in which these already existing burdens are multiplying themselves.

People around are tending to assume that your purpose in this universe is to act as an unpaid nursemaid, whose job it is to stand around all the time and be the psychological receptacle for their emotional garbage.

You have enough to do in your life without trying to live up to this martyr's role. In allowing others to treat you thus, you are only running away from where your true responsibilities lie. If you truly want to help others, then now you must turn round and refuse to allow yourself to be cast in this role. You will only really help them now by refusing to run around after them and making them accept responsibility for their own lives.

Now you must take courage to begin to say 'no' to people, and mean it. It doesn't really matter what they are asking you to do. Whether it is to stay on late and work overtime for nothing or whether it is to gain acceptance socially by contributing 'above and beyond the call of duty', your answer at this time must still be the same: 'NO.'

THE PAGE OF WANDS

This is a good time for you to achieve perspective in all possible senses of the word. It is a good time for education, either formal or informal, for getting in touch with yourself through self-awareness studies, or for seeing the larger world through travel.

Business and professional matters will be running quite smoothly at this time. Your relationships with people in positions of power are likely to be quite good and you may receive some kind of recognition for your achievements.

Your affairs in general seem to be running fairly smoothly and without apparent effort on your part. This is also a time when growth seems to take place in general – but especially in your own level of awareness. You can relax and take it easy for a while, knowing that your life is in good working order. People recognize the potential within you. In you, they see an aspect of themselves, albeit at a previous point in their lives. This is why they are being strangely and unaccountably generous towards you at this time. You can even attract powerful benefactors under this card!

THE KNIGHT OF WANDS

Here it is very important that you keep your affairs from getting out of hand. There is a strong tendency to excess, which may make it impossible to keep up with what you are involved in, simply because it is more than you can handle. Be particularly careful about financial matters, for you are likely to spend without thinking, confident that there is an abundance of money or other resources to back you up. You may not notice the pinch immediately, but after this influence is over, you may experience shortages that will be increased if you recklessly spend your money now.

But money isn't the only area of concern at this time. You may be over-committing yourself to projects that demand more time than you can afford. So in every area of your life, make sure that you really do have the time and energy to do what you have set out to do. Far better to tell people that you'd rather not take on any definite responsibilities than to have to admit later that you have been unable to do what you said you would do. Under these circumstances, it is better not to undertake anything for others than to undertake it and give only your second best.

THE QUEEN OF WANDS

If this card comes out in your reading, you are likely to feel good, with enough confidence and energy to handle just about anything. It is a period in your life when you feel optimistic and able to do whatever you want.

You must guard against over-confidence, though, so be careful that you don't take on more than you can handle.

This card helps to smooth over difficulties in your relationships, as well as to promote friendship and give you a strong desire for happy and peaceful times. You enjoy being with and talking with friends and will probably attend or hold several social gatherings during the coming period of time.

Events now, such as meetings with people or even psychological changes at a very deep level, are likely to be taking place. These situations will enable you to become wiser and more mature than before. This card can indicate that you are demanding more of the world and are less prepared to put up with second best.

Educational opportunities may well present themselves to you at this time or a chance to travel to a part of the world that you have never before seen, but which you have wanted to visit for a long time.

This is a good time to invest in your own inner resources, by doing counselling or by embarking on some personal programme of studies. But try not to over-commit your resources too far or to take on commitments that you may well find hard to fulfil at a later time.

THE KING OF WANDS

You are now inclined to do everything in a very big way. Your energy level is high and you are ambitious in everything that you do. You have a great need to expend physical energy, but be careful not to act recklessly. Discipline and restraint are vital at this time, no matter how much you may think otherwise.

Do not overestimate your abilities, either to yourself or to others. You are capable of doing quite a bit under this card, so you don't have to beat your own drum.

Don't take unnecessary chances. The feeling of omnipotence that this card confers is not real, at least not to the extent that you feel it.

On the other hand, this influence does confer real courage; the difference between this and foolhardiness is self-knowledge, which you must have in order to make this influence work out positively. If you are cool and collected in what you do, this will be a period of very considerable success.

The Suit of Cups

The suit of Cups represents the element Water and indicates feelings, reactions, desires, memories and hopes. The cup is a symbol of receiving, therefore this suit shows us how we can receive from others.

───────────── THE ACE OF CUPS ─────────────

A huge cup is being offered to you in this card, and you are being invited to reach out to grasp it and drink from it. What this cup is representing is a symbol of emotional fulfilment, not just on the emotional level, but on the spiritual level as well.

Whether you are going to reach out now and partake of this offering is going to depend obviously upon how thirsty you are, upon how much you are in need of being refreshed.

What this card is pointing at is the need for you to carefully define what it is that you want from the new offer of friendship or love which seems to have made its way into your life.

It may seem at first glance as though what you are being offered is what you have been waiting for: this card is saying that it is just a bit too early to be able to say. What you are going to have to do is wait and see.

Often this card comes up for someone who has just gone into a new relationship, or to whom an offer of love and/or friendship has been made. Or, it can simply mean that you are beginning to relate to people in a new and infinitely more responsive way – transcending much of the jealousy, possessiveness and emotional negativity of the past.

THE TWO OF CUPS

Here we are looking at two people coming together over a drink and raising their glasses in a toast to each other.

This could be the scene in which many different things begin to happen. It could be showing you entering a new relationship, either a love relationship or a business association of some kind.

The person who is meeting with you on this neutral territory is definitely someone who is interested in you; not just for the things which you represent, but in you yourself, as a personality.

The person who is symbolically in front of you could even be someone who has been in contact with you over an extended period of time. But in this case they have not, until now, revealed their interest in you.

Even at this point, they are being quite guarded, even coy, as to the extent of their interest.

Your best course of action is to play the whole situation at a very low key and not to take the whole thing either too seriously, or even to attribute too much significance to their interest. It is probably for the qualities which you are not aware of yourself that they are interested in you in the first place.

In this card, you are shown being reunited with friends from the past, possibly friends that you haven't seen for quite a long time. Or they may be new friends, with whom you feel a strong sense of affinity, a sense of having known them for ages.

What is happening here is that some kind of celebration is taking place around you and there is the real need for you to 'loosen up', relax and enjoy yourself at this time.

You have been very focalized up until now, concentrating on achieving in one or more of the areas of your interest. But you have become almost fanatical in the pursuit of your objectives.

Now, this card is saying, you must consciously and deliberately reverse this process, and take time out to brighten up your social life a little more.

Now is the time for you to get out there and meet people, to make more of an effort and be more open to some of the lighter, brighter, social influences which life is offering to you at this time.

Don't fall into any rigid mental pattern or attitude that what you are about to be shown is 'superficial' or 'meaningless'. It is not. It is simply a gentler colour in the emotional band of experience into which you are about to gain access.

In this card we are looking at someone sitting under a tree, looking at three cups, while a fourth is offered from the outside, held by a hand suspended in mid-air.

Your attention is very much focused on the people in your past who have been friends up until now, but from whom – in reality – you are experiencing little or no sense of emotional fulfilment. The cups from which you have been symbolically drinking have all run dry, and you are now unaware of where to go and what to do to begin to find happiness on a deeper level.

From a totally unexpected direction, new social contacts are about to open up for you.

Treasure these new people, for they are your doorway to a new and exciting chapter of social life and friendships which is opening up for you at this point. Their function will be a little unsettling at first, as you begin to absorb their influence, but go along with the new things which they will be showing you, for your life needs the new insights which they can provide.

─────────── THE FIVE OF CUPS ───────────

Here we see you standing in a dejected posture, looking at three cups which have been spilt, while behind you, out of sight, stand two upright cups which – in your dejection or disillusionment – you have failed to fully notice.

You are being warned here not to rely on the commitments or promises being made by those around you, especially on the emotional level. People are not deliberately attempting to deceive, but what is more likely is that they are getting carried away with their own naïve enthusiasm and projecting images of hope and fantasy above and far beyond their own capacity to provide.

This card is saying that you must not take these promises in too literal a sense. In fact, the best course of action for you is to remind these people that in reality you expect a lot less than they are offering.

In this way, when the going gets tough and it becomes increasingly difficult for them to deliver, they will be reminded of your words and make a far greater effort to make sure that what they have promised or are promising to you, will turn up on time and *become yours*.

THE SIX OF CUPS

With this card we see that your central lesson from life at this point is about how to give and receive on an emotional level in the kinds of relationships in which you are involved.

People are trying to share new things with you, and at this time you must be open to what they have to say and be less judgemental about the kinds of things which you feel they should be able to receive from you.

You are being shown here as something of a teacher – although you may not realize it yourself and may even feel a need to decry that aspect of your mission at this point. But others are increasingly coming to the conclusion that you have something important to say and that you deserve an audience.

Your message may or may not be known to you consciously, but it resonates with the lives of others and is having an impact on the way in which they are choosing to live.

At the same time, this card is warning you not to take yourself so seriously: recognize that others also have a teaching role and that they may in fact be discovering it through you. You have the potential to illuminate your own life and the lives of many others whose good fortune it is to have met you. Do so.

In this card we are looking at an incredible sense of confusion. All around you stand different cups – each one containing a symbol of some different objective, from something on the material plane to the emotional, the sexual or the spiritual. From each of the cups in this picture, we see a different symbol emerging: the dragon for wisdom, the snake for sexuality, the house for home and security, the jewels for wealth, the wreath for fame, the mask for identity and the face for relationships.

Suddenly, it is as though everything is being made open for you. But the sudden influence of all of these benefits coming to you in itself is overwhelming. Before this period of blessing is over, you will have to decide on two or possibly three main objectives that you wish to concentrate on.

If you try and grab everything which is seemingly presenting itself at this time, you will be failing to maximize the actual benefits of the present experience.

You must approach the present opportunities with a definite set of priorities and have your long-term objectives very carefully worked out.

If you are able to establish these conditions and establish mastery over the uncertainty of the present, then you will fare well out of this period of fantastic potential. If, however, you allow yourself to go into agreement with the prevailing illusions, then you will emerge from this influence with little to show from it.

—————————— THE EIGHT OF CUPS ——————————

In this card we see that you are being shown as a person who has turned away from a particular path in life and who has started off in a different direction. There is the sense that all you have built up in your life now has been shown to you as somehow lacking meaning, as lacking in fulfilment.

You have turned away from a lifestyle that was – to a great extent – based upon satisfying other people's desires or expectations. Now you are deeply concerned to find something on a far deeper, more fulfilling level.

You will do so, but you have a fair way to go to get back on the path that will lead you to where your true heart's desire may be found.

Don't expect that you will get to this deeper level of meaning easily. Certain superficial levels of your personality will be cleared away first. This is an important growth process in your life.

You are now being brought back to the direction your life has to take in order that your lifetime lessons may be more effectively learned. As your life comes back into alignment with your karmic destiny, you may first of all experience a sense of aloneness. It will seem that way at first. But, bit by bit, as you continue in your new direction, you will begin to meet others who are on the same new path as yourself. Basically, you are looking for something that is going to be deeply fulfilling; anything superficial is not going to work for you at all.

In this card we see you reaching a point where you are able not just to celebrate, but to experience life as a celebration in itself.

Now is the time you are able to say to yourself, 'Well done,' and give yourself a pat on the back. You have earned the recognition which you now enjoy from others. They see you increasingly as someone who has 'made it' in your own particular area of accomplishment. Your voice is heard by the people around you and your advice is acted upon.

You have within your potential at this time, the power to mobilise large numbers of people, to activate them, to get them out of their ruts in life. Around you others feel increasingly that they can rely on your sense of hospitality, that your presence alone provides the comfort and security in which their lives can begin to grow and expand.

Your role at this time is not just to enjoy yourself, but to avoid neglecting your role as host, as the person to whom destiny has entrusted the responsibility of ensuring that the creative potential of others should also receive encouragement.

Here the Tarot is saying that you should look around you and be aware of the abundance which life has brought into your lap. We have here the symbol of supreme emotional fulfilment, which for many people is often expressed through marriage with someone they are deeply in love with.

This particular expression may or may not apply to you, at least in a literal sense. But on a deeper level, there is a marriage of sorts taking place. And that is the marriage between your past and your future.

Now in your present you must be careful about the kinds of commitment you are entering into. More and more people will sense that you are on an upward-moving curve of increasing success, emotionally and materially.

With the sense of abundance and well-being that is now in your life, and which will be opening up even further in the coming period of activity, this card is saying that you must now go about sharing the blessings which have filtered into your life with those around you. But don't be discriminating as to whom you share those blessings with. Be generous, even with those people who have seemingly done little to deserve anything. The spirit of abundance which you bring into the lives of those around you will surely repay you many times over.

THE PAGE OF CUPS

At this time you are feeling more than usually optimistic and are able to proceed with the belief that everything will come out exactly as you want it to. And it probably will, because you don't get involved with grandiose thinking. Here, you have a reasonably good balance between details and generality in your thinking, but there is also a tendency to 'de-emphasize' the details and not pay adequate attention to them.

At this point, any dealings with the law should prove to be quite fortunate for you. You will prepare for any confrontation skilfully, leaving no loose ends to trip you up.

Often, this card comes up when someone is developing an interest in religious, spiritual or philosophical matters.

Communications with others are extremely fortunate under this influence. Your optimism and positive state of mind bring you good news from others concerning matters of importance.

Now is a great time for meeting new people, either socially or in connection with your work, who will help you to expand the perimeters of your life. Let them take you to places you don't normally go to, and to do things which you wouldn't normally find yourself doing. See yourself on a magic carpet, with them as your host or genie!

The emotional development of each person under this card is being looked at and the chance is given to realize that there is a greater amount of love in your life than at first realized. It is almost as though you no longer have to 'search for love' but rather relax back into your life, confident that you already have it.

It is also a very positive period to outflow this experience as well. Why not pick up the phone and tell other people just how much you feel for them?

The Knight is there to suggest action, but with regard to your emotions. It is a card which suggests that by being *bold* you might well attain the object of your affections. So, if you particularly fancy someone, now is the time to let them know something about it. It is no good keeping that information to yourself. People are not necessarily telepathic. Even after they are told something, they can only too easily forget.

On another level, this card points us towards questioning what it is that we want: what is it that attracts us to certain types and not others? And to what extent is the physical attraction the primary motive in any emotional union? Can we have love without sex? Can we have sex without love? What precisely do we experience from our inter-relationships? The Knight is a slightly adventurous symbol as well and is possibly pushing us to consider creating relationships the like of which may well have been outside the range of our normal periphery.

So, when this card comes up, think in terms of consciously establishing a relationship with someone who you wouldn't normally bother with.

So many times, when we walk into a room at, say, a party, we immediately blank most of the people there as an immediate psychological response, on whatever 'grounds'. And then we spend our time talking with people whose face fits the bill in some sense.

Well, the Knight is there to say, 'Hey! Become aware of what you're doing and try to override this tendency!'

THE QUEEN OF CUPS

You will be tending to feel quite positive and generous, and will be genuinely concerned about the welfare of those around you. You will be interested in the well-being and protection of those that you love.

You will find this to be a good time to be at home or in family surroundings. You will derive maximum support from being with your family and loved ones, for they will recharge your spirits.

At this point you will attract favourable circumstances and resources with seemingly little effort. Regardless of your own sex, you may very well benefit from heightened contact with women during this influence.

Some people, when this card reveals itself, can begin to undergo a greater interest in religious and spiritual thought. For many, this is one of the most deeply beautiful cards in the Tarot.

THE KING OF CUPS

This card is saying that you will enjoy being with and talking to friends and will probably hold or attend several social gatherings at this time. You may also be the centre of attention and will enjoy basking in the social limelight.

There may well be a new love interest in your life. Such a relationship under these conditions should prove to be an unusually successful one, in which you both grow a great deal, with an excellent balance of love and freedom. You will also be able to relate to loved ones with greater ease.

At this time, your taste is likely to become more elegant, and you may be tempted to buy something which is very expensive and fancy. Don't overdo it here – unless what you are buying really is going to be a fitting symbol of the love and affection which you feel.

Another possible problem to watch out for is the danger of self-indulgence at all levels, but particularly with food and drink. You may have a strong desire to surround yourself with beauty. You are concerned with the beautiful side of life at the moment and you should do all you can to expose yourself to it.

It may also be the case that you are able to act as a peacemaker between others – if so, don't underestimate the extent to which you can perform lasting service by stepping in and taking on the role of showing others how compromise can be achieved. Each person can accomplish more through negotiation than through conflict and destruction.

7

THE COURT CARDS

The Court cards show us the influential people in the Querent's life.

If we have Cups strongly represented, it would tend to emphasize the *emotional aspects* of these associations.

Wands would emphasize *doing, action*, what is to be done with these people.

Swords would show us how to look at areas of *possible conflict*, or where disconnections might have to be made.

Coins or Pentacles would be showing us *material, financial* aspects of these interconnections.

By looking at the surrounding cards, i.e. in the Minor Arcana, we can get a glimpse of how these connections can be established in a reading.

It is important to remember to work with the Querent and allow the cards to suggest areas in their life which need to be looked at – not in a dogmatic way, in which we try to define the Querent's life strictly by the cards which have come up for them in a reading, but by allowing ourselves some flexibility in how we piece all of these powerful symbols together.

For example, in a man's cards, the Knight of Coins could show him in relation to his present work, or his future plans for work, or could even prompt him to question what he sees himself doing, say, a few years down the line. It could be asking him to define his own objectives.

In a woman's cards, the same card might suggest questions as to how she gets on with men associates, if she sees herself as sufficiently empowered to hold her own against male competitors, or it might be identified by her as pertaining to a specific person active in her work scenario in the present. It could be linked tentatively with the material objectives she shares with her partner (e.g. buying property, a car, going on holiday). It could be asking her to look at how she shares the costs of running a home with her partner or suggesting some possible business activity which might involve them more closely together.

It could be showing an Earth aspect of the relationship with this man, it could suggest the physical, the concrete, or the more tangible aspects of the reality which she shares with this figure. If the Querent is a man, it could further represent him or a male figure in his life. For a woman it could also represent the male or active side of her life, or a need for her to use this side of herself in certain matters.

So you see that there will always be so many possible ways in which the Court cards can be linked in with the tapestry of the Querent's life which you will see unfolding before you in a Tarot spread.

After a fairly short time, you will be surprising yourself at the speed and flexibility with which you can race around and make all of these connections fluidly and immediately.

You are probably thinking that there are many possible permutations which can be made. But if you were to look at a map of a city which you had never been to before, you wouldn't sit there and say, 'I could easily get lost because there are so many possible streets I could wander down', because the map is there to guide you.

Well, this is really what you have in the Querent's Tarot spread. A map. And just as a map actually looks totally unlike the physical reality of what it represents, so a Tarot spread looks unlike the life of the person whose cards you are reading. But it is down to you as the reader to make sense of what is being shown there.

At first some of the symbols may seem confused, or jumbled together, or altogether out of place. But they are there for a reason, whether it is obvious at first or not. Similarly, it is easy to make a mistake and assign too much significance to just one or two symbols without having the experience to place everything in a realistic perspective.

There is no way around each of these pitfalls: you will have to go through each of them at one time or another.

With the Court cards you will have the chance to touch upon the personality influences of the Querent and look at how their relationships are functioning, in the aspects of work, emotion, conflict, and activity.

The Queen of Cups in a woman's spread will show either her or a woman who is significant in some way in her life. It shows her emotional side and indicates significance in this domain. If the Querent is a man, such a card will tend to shed some light on how he relates to women. Is he honest with them? Does he use them or is he open about what he wants from his associations with them? This card would point the reader in the direction of intuiting about his 'track record' in relationships. Does he possess any relationship skills, is he an effective communicator, does he even know what he wants from a woman? These would be some of the possible areas for you to look at.

Court cards of the suit of Swords are not necessarily 'bad cards', although the artwork on some of them is a bit frightening! When they turn up in a Querent's spread they show how conflict with others is experienced. Is the person an honest and open 'fighter'? Or are they more manipulative, hoping to achieve better results through more indirect means? Are their relationships marked by periods of sudden upheaval and turmoil, or have they developed the means to become more causative and direct in their relationships and associations with others? The Knight of Swords in a man's spread could show either his combative side or a man whom he is in conflict with. It could even show inner conflict: a man driven by two opposing desires, for example. It could show that the man tends to look upon his life a series of never-ending battles, and creates his own enemies and problems as a result. Taken in this way, it might indicate the need for him to look upon others as bringing positive things to him, for him to consciously try and develop a greater sense of the basic goodness in others.

In a woman's cards it would tend to show a man that she has had or is having certain problems with. This could be on a number of levels: at work, a neighbour, a guy who won't take 'no' for an answer. It could show a male figure in her family that she has had a lot of problems with: an abusive father, a father that she never really knew, or a brother that she wants to help but who won't let himself receive any.

Court cards of the suit of Wands will prompt the reader to look for ways in which the Querent can become more 'at-cause' and less 'at-effect' of life. At-cause means being able to take the initiative and not so afraid of failure (or success, even). It means not waiting around for someone else to do something to get things in motion. It means acting as a trigger for events, being a spark, being prepared to stand out and stand up for whatever is believed in and felt to be right and good. People who have strong beliefs and who are fighting causes will often be shown in a Querent's spread as Wand characters.

REVERSALS

Court card reversals will tend to show extreme of excessive aspects of the qualities touched upon by the card(s) concerned. The person shown as 'dynamic and enervating' as the Knight or Queen of Wands may thus be tyrannical, bullying, dogmatically attuned to one single area or interpretation of life. Such a person may be unreasonable and incapable of compromise.

A reversed Cup Court card may show someone whose feelings are all over the place, who is in love one day and out the next. Conversely, it may show someone who is afraid to love, who can't bear the thought of risking being hurt and who therefore rejects every even vague possibility of friendship with others before they are rejected. A reversed Sword Court card may not differ much from its normal, upright meaning, but a reversed Coin Court card would point the reader in the direction of looking to see if the people thus represented were actually in touch with basic economic realities of life. They might need help in ascertaining their priorities or guidance in how they might clarify their goals and the way in which they might achieve them.

8

CONCENTRATED MEANINGS

In the Heightened Meanings we looked at the expanded meaning of each card. We looked at how each card opens up. Here, in the Concentrated Meanings, we are going to look at how each card comes to life, and how it links with astrological and other phenomena in the world.

MAJOR ARCANA
0 THE FOOL

DESCRIPTION OF CARD

A young man meanders along, with a knapsack on his back, holding in one hand a white rose, emblematic of the purity of his intention. He is completely absorbed in his own world and is unaware of the danger in his surroundings.

By his side, a small dog scurries, barking at him, trying to warn him of what lies ahead. A few paces ahead, he will come to a cliff edge. Will he waken in time or is his seeming oblivion just a false impression?

On the side of his knapsack we see the 12 astrological signs, suggesting that although he travels light, he really carries with him everything he needs.

THE FOOL SPEAKS

'I am the Fool, so some say! But look at those who criticise me! Stuck in their lives of boredom and monotony, never daring to get in touch with what I represent! All that I am doing is in truth refusing to follow other people; why should we blindly carry out the orders of others and their conventions? Life can be so much more exciting and interesting when you let me loose in your lives and start taking down your own barriers. I am all that is original, inventive and different. Eccentricity is something to be praised.

The gypsies knew me, travelling around all over the world, carrying all their belongings wherever they went. They never worried where or how they were going to make money. They trusted life to bring to them all that they needed. The hippies and the travellers of more recent years had something of me also; although they started to establish their own little hierarchies in place of the ones they sought to be free from.

Be young, be adventurous! If you stay in your truth, you'll stay in your youth! Why grow old and die!'

ASTROLOGICAL ASSOCIATION

Uranus – planet of originality, eccentricity and the unpredictable. Previously, the Air element.

DIVINATORY MEANING

A time to take the initiative, to be different, to emphasize your own individuality.

Look around and see where you might be following what was appropriate for someone else. Become more aware of how others' expectations may be playing a role in your plans. A good time to start out on something completely different. A time to take on more – expand your limitations!

BULLET MEANING

A new chapter in life opening up for you.

WORLDLY ASSOCIATIONS

Gypsies, hippies, travellers. Nomads of all kinds. Aboriginals. University drop-outs. Mystics.

POSITIVE QUALITY

Freedom for the individual.

NEGATIVE QUALITY

Refusal to accept responsibilities. 'It's not my problem.'

1 THE MAGICIAN

DESCRIPTION OF CARD

A man stands in a courtyard, demonstrating his conjuring ability to passers-by. His is the gift of the gab, to keep people interested in what he is saying long enough to get them interested in what he is doing. On the table in front of him we see various artifacts which are part of his stock-in-trade. In particular, a Coin or Pentacle, representing Earth, a Cup for Water, a Wand for Fire and a Sword for Air.

Each of the four elements is at his command. He can move from one state of being to another. He moves easily in different worlds and probably has friends from many different walks of life. He holds one arm upraised while the other points down to the ground, symbolizing the bringing down of spiritual power into the material world. 'As above, so below.'

THE MAGICIAN SPEAKS

'Step right this way, hurry, hurry, hurry! Come and see what I have to offer you today! I am the Magician, and I am the epitome of all salesmen and advertising people. OK, so yesterday wasn't so brilliant and today's not even special, but tomorrow is going to be golden! I represent the advertiser's dream, which is that the future is always going to be better than the past. I am the symbol of communication and without me you can't sell what you've made, you can't even talk to one another about your feelings! The ancient Romans worshipped me in the form of Mercury and invoked me whenever they wanted to improve their trade – or just get a message from one part of the Empire to another. I command travel as well and rule over all forms of transportation, especially by air. Be careful, not everything that I suggest you'll be able to take as gospel. In my negative aspect I can sweet-talk little old ladies out of their life savings and then just vanish! Now you see me, now you don't! Well, at least I'll take the initiative and chance my arm! Why don't you? You might come out lucky!'

ASTROLOGICAL ASSOCIATION

Mercury – planet of communication, study and speedy movement.

DIVINATORY MEANING

A pointer towards increasing your communication with others. Tell them, don't just keep it to yourself. You can't assume that they know what you're thinking, what it is that you want. A pointer towards any kind of study or learning. Teaching of one kind or another is shown here, maybe in a formal setting or otherwise. Thinking of travelling? Why not? What's holding you back?

BULLET MEANING

The need to put your message across to a wider audience.

WORLDLY ASSOCIATIONS

Advertisers, salesmen, promoters. Gamblers, financiers, risk-takers of any kinds. International relations, translators. Good communicators, teachers, assiduous students.

POSITIVE QUALITIES

Initiative, good teaching. Order, everything defined and labelled. Research well done. Reasonable, truthful, dispassionate. Thorough.

NEGATIVE QUALITIES

Tricksters, conmen. Lies, half-truths. Able to justify anything.

2 THE HIGH PRIESTESS

DESCRIPTION OF CARD

A woman stands in a temple, dressed in the robes of the officiating High Priestess. She is a woman of power, but by her gentle demeanour she obviously doesn't have to over-exert her authority in order to get things done.

In her hands she is opening a scroll, which contains certain mystical secrets only half-perceived by us as yet.

In her headband we see the three phases of the Moon, suggestive of growth, preservation and decay.

At her feet we see a crescent Moon, showing us that she rules over the instinctual nature, our subconscious minds and our dreams.

Behind her we can get an impression of the sea, reminding us of the greatness of the power which she represents.

THE HIGH PRIESTESS SPEAKS

'I am the force of the female and without me your lives will be dry like the desert. Your reason and logic are only very recently developed qualities of your mind. They came into existence when first you began working with the Magician and in his cleverness he showed you how to write, make tools, weapons, lay traps for animals, make ploughs and then ships.

But before he came along I was with you during those many millions of years. It was my intuition within you that gave you the knowledge of when something was safe and when it wasn't, of when a wild beast was just around the corner, even though with your physical senses you couldn't perceive it.

Even now, without me you couldn't survive for long, because I tell you what your other senses cannot pick up on. You think all those millionaires have made their money just on the Magician's logic alone? Think again, because without me they would never have intuited when to hold back and when to have taken the gamble. How ironic that those that rely on me the most so often give me the least credence!'

ASTROLOGICAL ASSOCIATION

The Moon – the 'mother', the 'trigger', which brings into fruition all the latent conditions.

DIVINATORY MEANING

Reflect on what you have been going through. Learn to see your life in terms of tides: inflow and outflow. Use your mind as a mirror. You have all the knowledge you are going to need. Now you must let the knowledge you already have filter through from your subconscious to your conscious.

BULLET MEANING

Be guided by your intuition.

WORLDLY ASSOCIATIONS

Mothers, psychics, intuitives. Women teachers. Carers.

POSITIVE QUALITIES

Telepathic, empathic. Survivalist.

NEGATIVE QUALITIES

Reactive. Located in the past. Hocus-pocus. Superstitions. Fears of what lies 'out there'.

--- 3 THE EMPRESS ---

DESCRIPTION OF CARD

A woman sits in a green pasture, by the side of a flowing river. The greenness of her surroundings suggests growth and the entire scene is one of harmony.

Around her grow different flowers, suggesting pollination, and the reproductive cycle.

The woman herself is pregnant, large enough to indicate that childbirth is not far away. In her arm she holds a shield, indicating that she still has her defences around her. At her feet rests a crescent Moon, showing that the growth processes which she represents are still based on certain rhythmic patterns in the universe.

Between her breasts she bears her heart surmounted by a cross, showing that her spiritual power is that of love.

THE EMPRESS SPEAKS

'I am the Empress, rightly called, for my power is that of love and love is all. So great is my power that men and women have died in my honour. Rather than have them die, I would prefer that they let my force transform them. I rule over all growth in nature and that includes childbirth. What is the power of man next to the power of woman which gives birth to them? I am the mother of all, but not all that I give birth to will survive. I am Mother Nature, constantly creating new forms of life in experimentation. In the wild, nothing survives unless it is capable of proving worthy of the life which I bestow to it. I am not as gentle as I may seem. There is more to Nature than a summer's day in the park. In my capacity as goddess of love I have seen terrible crimes committed in my name, but in reality those who commit such crimes do not know me. What blasphemy!'

ASTROLOGICAL ASSOCIATION

Venus – planet of love, harmony, natural forces.

DIVINATORY MEANING

The representation is of harmony, which doesn't necessarily show that that is what you are experiencing. But it suggests that you look at how that can realistically be achieved. In terms of creating, the card is asking what it is that you are hoping to create; how and for what do you wish to harness your creativity?

BULLET MEANING

The need to cultivate your own creativity.

WORLDLY ASSOCIATIONS

Nature, mothers, pregnancy, nature, artists, writers, actors, theatre.

POSITIVE QUALITIES

Loving, harmonious, peaceful, gentle. Able to reconcile opposites. Diplomatic. Charming.

NEGATIVE QUALITIES

Too compromising. Too easy-going. Not sufficiently self-assertive.

————————— 4 THE EMPEROR —————————

DESCRIPTION OF CARD

A man sits on a throne, his head bowed slightly as if he is about to make an important decision or pass judgement. In one hand he holds a sceptre, while in the other he holds an orb; the orb represents his capacity for mercy, while the sceptre shows his capacity to punish. His robe is reminiscent of that worn by the Roman Emperor.

His entire demeanour suggests that he is to be taken seriously. His visage is severe and it would be unwise to get on the wrong side of him. He could be a strong ally in times of need, though.

THE EMPEROR SPEAKS

'I am the Emperor and what I say goes. I am in charge here, because your level of development tells me that you cannot be trusted to be left to your own devices. Your tendency to evil is still strong and wherever you can get away with it you commit crimes against each other. That is why you still need laws and the firm hand of fatherly punishment when you overstep the mark. At times I have been excessively harsh, I admit. But as you can see from the orb which I hold in my left hand, if I feel that the wrong-doer has made a genuine mistake and wishes to change his ways, then I will show mercy. Getting a balance between these two is difficult, but it is my job. Sometimes I go too far the other way and allow someone who has committed really horrendous crimes to walk freely back into society where they can continue their activities.

I also represent the self-made person. So many women now have an essence of me in their personalities. No longer prepared to allow their menfolk sway over their destinies, they are reclaiming their own power and achieving their own independence. Although I stand for established order now, for most of my early life I was a rebel against the injustices of the then order of things. In fact, this throne which you see me sitting on didn't come to me by any hereditary title. No, I took it, by the power of my own sword, from a corrupt and useless ruler who sat on it before me!'

ASTROLOGICAL ASSOCIATION

Aries – cardinal sign of Fire. Leadership.

DIVINATORY MEANING

The card points to our own dynamism, our own capacity to give ourselves a boot up the backside and get things together. No point in waiting around for other people to do things for us. We are the masters of our own destiny. No point in blaming others; that will just be a transfer of power over to them. Let's raise the energy level and get some action going! If we have to take some tough decisions, then so be it! Life, after all, is war!

BULLET MEANING

The struggle to achieve your own independence.

WORLDLY ASSOCIATIONS

Men and women of action. Leaders. Heroes and heroines. Joan of Arc. Revolutionaries. Trail-blazers.

POSITIVE QUALITIES

Old, out-of-date patterns thrown over. New possibilities. Self-respect through self-sufficiency.

NEGATIVE QUALITIES

Harsh, no second chance. Overly severe. Militaristic. Combative even when not called for. Excessive penalties.

---

5 THE HIEROPHANT

DESCRIPTION OF CARD

A man stands in a darkened temple room, dressed in his ceremonial robes, performing some act of initiation. He is clearly very senior in the order to which he is a member. It is as though he is telling us something, possibly revealing to us some mystical passwords or signs, through which we will make ourselves known to other members of the order. He stands as though giving a speech, almost as if the speech itself were a liturgy or had to be remembered by heart. On either side of the Hierophant stand two pillars, one representing the masculine or celestial regions, the other the feminine or terrestrial.

THE HEIROPHANT SPEAKS

'I am the Hierophant and it is my honour to officiate at your initiation. Today we are able to welcome you into our order and bestow upon you the blessing which that membership entails. Never forget that your commitment to us shall be binding for as long as you shall live and that you will be bound by the decisions which we shall take. Entrusted to you now are the mystical signs, seals and secrets which you shall know us by, in particular, the crossed keys which you see before you. Together they represent the master–disciple relationship; the silver key represents your own desire for knowledge, the golden key represents that which your Master can open for you. And the two conjoined together represent your desire for knowledge and that of your Master linking together. I particularly commend to you a study of our ancient traditions, for in them you will find the answers to your questions; in particular, how you may lead a happy and fulfilled life.

ASTROLOGICAL ASSOCIATION

Taurus – fixed sign of Earth. Worldly possessions, traditions.

DIVINATORY MEANING

A time when teachers – or just teaching – will be coming into your life. But they cannot force their way in. You will get from them what you are able to receive. Be open, be receptive. It may also be a time when life will be bringing new people into your world and asking you to take the responsibility of teaching them about the things which you have learnt. A time when that which has been hidden from you for a long time becomes open. But respect for what you now find open is going to be important.

BULLET MEANING

Important teacher. This could be the Querent or someone coming into the Querent's life.

WORLDLY ASSOCIATIONS

Builders, masons. Establishment. Ethics. Responsibilities. Traditionalists, in both positive and negative associations.

POSITIVE QUALITIES

Continuity. Tolerance. Standards. Principles. Charitable acts.

NEGATIVE QUALITIES

Conspiracy. Secrets. Crimes concealed. Black-listing. Judgemental. Conformist.

6 THE LOVERS

DESCRIPTION OF CARD

Two people stand embracing each other. They seem to be so complete, almost as if they were two facets of the same person.

Around them we see dense foliage, suggestive of the creative force of nature. The sun beats down its rays strongly upon the Earth, symbolizing the Father's interaction with the Mother. Great emotional intensity is shown here. The two lovers look into each other's eyes, as if plumbing the depths of each other's soul.

THE LOVERS SPEAK

'We are the Lovers, united by the emotion we feel for each other. United means brought together as one; no longer are we the two separate halves of which so many other couples are composed. What we have found in each other is the envy of the world. That is why people go crazy when two people fall in love, trying to bust it up or get in the way of the relationship successfully developing.

We are like two halves who have found their way back to each other after many lifetimes of being separated. Many try to avoid discovering their own wholeness by desperately flinging themselves into a relationship with another. Hence the word "fling". It has often been said that you must love yourself before another can, and there is much truth in this. To look for love from another before you have come to know, understand, accept and love yourself is like running without having first tied your shoelaces. It's not impossible, but it is just possible that you could trip over.

Every true love must go through a testing time; when the trust, faith and belief in each other will be placed on the anvil, and its true worth seen for what it is.'

ASTROLOGICAL ASSOCIATION

Gemini – mutable sign of Air. Duality.

DIVINATORY MEANING

Raises issues concerning your relationships with others. Is there enough love in your life? How would you like to see more? Are you giving out love so that you might get it back? What kind of people do you tend to select as possible partners?

The card refers to emotional intensity and therefore commitments. Are you interested in establishing commitments or do you just want to have a good time?

BULLET MEANING

Intensity – and choices – in relationships.

WORLDLY ASSOCIATIONS

All those involved in loving relationships. The sexually active.

Those who have to choose who they are going to be with.

POSITIVE QUALITIES

The beauty of love and sexual fulfilment.

NEGATIVE QUALITIES

Promiscuity. Guilt. Venereal diseases. AIDS.

---

7 THE CHARIOT

DESCRIPTION OF CARD

A man drives a chariot at great speed, holding the reins of power tightly in his hands. His chariot is pulled by two horses, one white, the other black. They symbolize opposite qualities of his personality, over which he has been strong enough to make them pull in the same direction. A sense of great momentum is here, of irresistible force. On his shoulders are two crescent moons, feminine symbols, while on his breastplate is the Sun, a masculine symbol. On his head he wears the sign of three stars.

THE CHARIOT SPEAKS

'I am the Chariot and as you can see I am rushing past you on my way to even greater victory! I have achieved one of the greatest of victories already, in that I have learned how to balance my masculine and feminine. Many have misunderstood this concept and have confused the esoteric teaching in this with their own unresolved contradictions. In fact the teaching is how we achieve empowerment through being alternately active and passive, much as the tide is sometimes inflowing and then outflowing. In fact, if you look really closely at my belt, you will be able to see the astrological symbol of Cancer, which is a reference to the principle of tides and currents which I have just revealed to you.

With me, you have the ability to advance when you have the opportune conditions and the knowledge of when to hold back until the situation changes again in your favour.

By my strong mastery over the horses which I drive – in other words, my own desire nature – I am able to fix my mind upon that which I wish to attain and move rapidly towards those goals.'

ASTROLOGICAL ASSOCIATION

Cancer – cardinal sign of Water. Caring, nurturing.

DIVINATORY MEANING

Great speed, movement, is being shown here. You must hold tightly onto your reins of power and maintain a sense of forward momentum. The race is on!

BULLET MEANING

Keep your concentration on your present objectives; don't change horses in midstream.

WORLDLY ASSOCIATIONS

Bringing up children, as against just giving birth to them. Targets, objectives. Protective. Social services.

POSITIVE ASSOCIATIONS

Caring, motherly, sincere.

NEGATIVE ASSOCIATIONS

Apron-strings, restrictive. Restrictive, domineering.

---

8 STRENGTH

DESCRIPTION OF CARD

A woman stands by the side of a lion, effortlessly opening or closing its mouth with her hand. Her face is serene, showing that she accomplishes this awesome task without any apparent effort. In her hands the lion is almost docile.

STRENGTH SPEAKS

'I am Strength and in me you see how the lower aspects of man's nature may be commanded by the force of reason. The lion which you see me effortlessly holding is a symbol of the emotional nature of humanity, which is still basically wild, usually held back by the fear of the Emperor or the traditions of the Hierophant. With me you begin to get the first hint as to how we can begin to transcend our own tendency towards base emotionalism, through its distillation into spiritual awareness. With me you have a constant supporter in your quest for spiritual growth. There is little that can be achieved – in the long run – through self-restraint. Admittedly, the Emperor is needed, because at your present level of development you still need laws and rules to protect the weak and helpless. But it is I who shows you the direction which you must take in the long run.'

DIVINATORY MEANING

A pointer towards exercising your qualities of reason, rather than to respond with anger, injured pride or feelings of self-importance. The lion on his own can be a very destructive force, but when feelings are brought under the jurisdiction of the mind, then something much more positive can be derived.

ASTROLOGICAL ASSOCIATION

Leo – fixed sign of Fire. Pride, magnanimity.

BULLET MEANING

Let your head rule your heart, *not* the other way round.

WORLDLY ASSOCIATIONS

The rights of man. The UN Declaration.

POSITIVE ASSOCIATIONS

Self-esteem, respect for the rights of others. The dignity of one's fellow-creatures.

NEGATIVE ASSOCIATIONS

No checks or balances. Power concentrated in too few hands.

-------------------- 9 THE HERMIT --------------------

DESCRIPTION OF CARD

We see a lone figure of an elderly man, standing against the backdrop of a mountain range at night. The scene is one of darkness and a cold wind seems to be blowing from one direction. Around by his feet and on the tops of mountains behind him we can see snow. In his hand he holds a lamp, from which a six-pointed star is shining. His light represents the inner light of wisdom, which is revealed through meditation and quiet contemplation.

THE HERMIT SPEAKS

'I am the Hermit and sooner or later you will have to know me. I represent the initial contacts which you will have with your own inner light of wisdom. Your first encounter with me may well be quite by chance, when you hear a non-spoken voice talking to you. I say non-spoken because any "voice" which you otherwise "hear" in any clairaudient sense is the result of mental circuitry going off in the wrong direction. But when I speak to you, you will know it with a greater certainty than you could possibly visualize at this time. I am that light which stands in the darkness, showing you that the way to spiritual truth lies in the opposite direction to the sense of gratification of the material world. Many mystics have realized this, that to get to that inner light they must first of all still the clamouring of the senses for yet more sensation. Thus they have renounced their wealth, have put on sackcloth, have taken up a diet of plain-tasting food. But so beautiful has been the connection which they have made with their own divine light that all of these other "pleasures" have seemed mere dross in comparison, mere wrapping paper.'

ASTROLOGICAL ASSOCIATION

Virgo – mutable sign of Earth. Critical, analytical.

DIVINATORY MEANING

The Hermit shows us one possible way towards liberation of the human soul, rather than necessarily the only way in which that is achieved. Thus he could well lead us out of the rocky pass we find ourselves in. But we shouldn't be too quick to avail ourselves of what he offers us in its place.

Caution is advised here, even if we do choose to follow his lead and take the path of renunciation which he suggests. Essentially, we shouldn't rush at this point. Let us instead look at what other options there might be.

BULLET MEANING

Don't rush into new sets of commitments. Look before you leap.

WORLDLY ASSOCIATIONS

Ashrams, monasteries, nunneries. Places of refuge. The mountains. Tibet. Caves. Buddhist monks. Devotees.

POSITIVE QUALITIES

Meditation, serenity, realization, enlightenment. Transcendence. Needing little materially.

NEGATIVE QUALITIES

Withholding. Puritanical. Condemnatory of the pleasures of others. Spiritual pride.

———————— 10 THE WHEEL OF FORTUNE ————————

DESCRIPTION OF CARD

A great wheel is seen turning. A huge hand – the hand of God or of fate – is seen to be responsible. Around the rim of the wheel we can see people at various stages of life's experience. At the top, we see a man and a woman toasting each other, seemingly unaware that they are just about to begin their descent downward, thus showing that their fortunes seem to be on the wane. While at the bottom, we see someone who has already come down as far as he can getting thrown off the wheel altogether.

THE WHEEL OF FORTUNE SPEAKS

'I am the Wheel of Fortune and in me you can discover how to avoid going through the ups and downs of life, or at the very least how to prepare for those changing times and seasons so that they will not have so much of an impact on you when they do occur.

Basically, when you find yourself in "summer", in other words in a condition of abundance, it is then that you should act with thought for "winter", i.e. when scarcity will be the order of the day. And when you find yourself in "winter", then get ready with all your seeds for when springtime comes along and you can get planting again.

This teaching you can apply to any situation of human life, be it in relationships or in your business or working life!'

ASTROLOGICAL ASSOCIATION

Jupiter – planet of abundance, faith, hope.

DIVINATORY MEANING

Abundance is the keyword here, but it is directly related to your faith, your hope, your optimism. The need to think on a bigger scale; to think not just of the next project, but the next 100 projects! A person ultimately gets only what they truly expect. So let's make your expectation higher, so that we can get some bigger and better results!

BULLET MEANING

Abundance, but still pay attention to the details!

WORLDLY ASSOCIATIONS

The priesthood. Optimists. Philanthropists. Sharers. Co-operative ventures.

POSITIVE QUALITIES

Generosity. The world is your oyster. No limitation. The sky's the limit!

NEGATIVE QUALITIES

Excessive use of intoxicants. Over-funding. Over-expenditure. Huge debts. Expense account. Massive mortgage.

—————————— 11 JUSTICE ——————————

DESCRIPTION OF CARD

A robed figure stands facing us, in one hand a sword upraised, emblematic that justice will be done, while in the other hand the scales of justice are seen, not yet in the process of having achieved a balance.

The card shows the law of cause and effect; the law of karma.

JUSTICE SPEAKS

'I am Justice and I show myself in many forms, not all of them equally obviously.

I am not especially related to social conventions of justice, as these change continuously in accordance with the societies which they come from.

I am the law of cause and effect which, simply stated, is that you will get back what you give out. Any genuine spiritual teacher will teach this, however unpopular it may be with the society which he or she comes from.

One of the strongest illusions of the material plane is that you can escape me or, in other words, that you can escape from the ripples in the water which you yourself have created.

Oftentimes, it may seem as though an injustice is committed in the world; the guilty go free on a technicality or the innocent are not protected. But this is another illusion of the material plane. Some believe that if you could see behind the veil of past incarnations which I stand in front of, you would see that when a guilty soul receives seemingly undeserved mercy in this lifetime, it is from some positive deed carried out previously. And vice versa: when a seemingly innocent soul undergoes apparent injustice, it is the cancelling out of some karmic debt from before.

But only I know whether this is true or not, or whether it is just their way of blinkering themselves to the things which need changing in the world.'

ASTROLOGICAL ASSOCIATION

Libra – cardinal sign of Air. Achieving a balance.

DIVINATORY MEANING

How do you achieve a balance in your life between what you want and how you can get it? Between what you are giving out to yourself and what you are giving to others? If you feel that the balance is too firmly slanting the wrong way, then it is up to you to redress the imbalance by leaning in the opposite direction!

BULLET MEANING

Attempting to achieve a state of harmony.

WORLDLY ASSOCIATIONS

Negotiators, counsellors, therapists. Body-workers. Representatives.

POSITIVE QUALITIES

Agreement, accord. Truce. Ceasefire.

NEGATIVE QUALITIES

Stalemate. Indecision. Vacillation. Dithering.

——————— 12 THE HANGED MAN ———————

DESCRIPTION OF CARD

A man hangs upside down from a tree, with one foot tying him there. From his face we see that he isn't in any obvious pain. With one foot crossed over the other and his arms crossed behind his back he is making a series of triangles with his body, which is emblematic of the symbol of Water, the element of purification. Hanging by one foot for a day was at one time a punishment meted out to criminals.

THE HANGED MAN SPEAKS

'I am the Hanged Man, strung up here as a punishment. Actually, I don't much mind, because it gives me the chance to see things from a new perspective.

It is interesting to invert commonly-held truths, because sometimes by looking at things from an upside-down perspective, we can get a glimpse as to how we can change things over.'

ASTROLOGICAL ASSOCIATION

Neptune – planet of dreams, illusions. Water element, emotions, feelings.

DIVINATORY MEANING

Don't be so self-sacrificial. A period of temporary suspension of activities. Lots of hang-ups. Being blown around by the winds of public opinion.

BULLET MEANING

Overly self-sacrificial; too helpful.

WORLDLY ASSOCIATIONS

Dreamers, idealists. Impractical types.

POSITIVE QUALITIES

Unselfish. Vows of poverty. Vows of obedience. Psychotherapy. Self-analysis.

NEGATIVE QUALITIES

Too self-absorbed. Too wrapped up in one's own problems. Hidden resentment. Covert hostility.

---

13 DEATH

DESCRIPTION OF CARD

The skeleton of Death stands before us, holding the scythe in its hands. Behind it runs the river of life, which separates the living from the dead. Looking at the whiteness of the head of Death and the curve of the scythe, we can almost see a yin-yang symbol of change being hinted at in this card, suggestive of the flux and change of energy from one form to another.

DEATH SPEAKS

'I am Death. Just as in life, some people and situations have turned out to be the exact opposite of what they initially seemed. So am I. I represent *rebirth* – new positive influences coming into being and the clearing away of all that has become outmoded. Sometimes, from a sense of attachment, you may well want to hold onto that which is no longer of any value to you. That may be a belief, a conviction or a sense about yourself. I am here to help you discard those old conditions which will only hold you back. Just as a snake discards its old skin, so each of us at times must discard aspects of our former selves and previous lifestyles. How can we move on and develop in our lives, if we try and carry everything which we have brought with us from the past? We cannot 'carry' every former friend, for example, for if we did we would never have any impulse to make new friends. We cannot remain stuck in old patterns, because if we do we will become outdated and unable to keep up with the tempo of life in the present. Any business that is unable to keep up with new developments will soon find itself bankrupt. Any country which tries to run itself along outdated and inflexible political lines soon finds itself with a revolution on its hands. That which was true for us once may no longer be. That which is true for us now may not be in the future. I am here to show you these things!'

ASTROLOGICAL ASSOCIATION

Scorpio – fixed sign of Water. Intensity.

DIVINATORY MEANING

The Death card shows that one complete period of your life is coming to a close, to make way for a new one which is beginning. We see here the cosmic street-sweeper, clearing away all the debris to make way for new life forms to come along. Without that process of purification, that new life would just get choked out and be denied its chance of existence.

BULLET MEANING

The clearing away of negative conditions to make way for new, more positive ones to arrive.

WORLDLY ASSOCIATIONS

Surgeons. The Official Receiver. Inherited goods.

POSITIVE ASSOCIATIONS

Release of old energy. Liberation from the body. Cessation of disease. Light at the end of the tunnel.

NEGATIVE ASSOCIATIONS

The trauma of going through with something. Pain at the dentists. Adapting to new conditions.

14 TEMPERANCE

DESCRIPTION OF CARD

An angel stands before us, pouring water from one cup to another, without spilling a drop. The angel is a symbol of healing. It stands with one foot on the ground and the other on water, thus symbolizing that its power bridges the elements. It is pouring the water from one glass to the other as a way of measuring out how much needs to be given. For one cup has been used in collecting the water from the stream, while the other is to be used by us for drinking out of.

THE ANGEL SPEAKS

'I am the angel, sometimes called Michael, sometimes called Raphael, depending on who precisely is talking about me. I am a direct servant of God and my function is that of healing. What you see me doing here in this picture is actually collecting water to mix with mud. With this mud I am going to go and cure the eyes of a man suffering from blindness. In a sense, you might be that person, because although you may partially see, yet you do not fully. I represent healing in all its forms. It is noteworthy that before He healed anyone, Jesus would always ask them whether they wanted to be healed. If they replied in the affirmative, he would get them to do something, such as stretch out their hand. Something, no matter how small. Because implicit in this was the symbol that they were doing something to help themselves, that they were taking a first step in their own healing process.

That first step is what I represent, which is why you see one of my feet in the water and the other having taken a symbolic first step onto land. So likewise, if you would be healed also, I would have you stretch out your hand, symbolically, and actively seek out the healing processes which are available.

In the open road behind me, you see the road which lies behind each and every one of us. So, any process of healing will involve us looking back into that road and seeing what has happened there from a fresh perspective.'

ASTROLOGICAL ASSOCIATION

Sagittarius – mutable sign of fire. Freedom.

DIVINATORY MEANING

Gaining self-understanding, as you find yourself able to confront the past. A process of moving from one level of maturity to another.

BULLET MEANING

Looking into the past, so that you can better understand your present.

WORLDLY ASSOCIATIONS

Self-development, channelling. Broadening one's perspectives. Travelling, freedom of movement.

POSITIVE QUALITIES

Depth of understanding. Ability to embrace different realities. Hope, breath of fresh air. Inspirational influence.

NEGATIVE INFLUENCE

Overlooking pitfalls. Not centred. Little foundation. Dispersed energy pattern.

---

15 THE DEVIL

DESCRIPTION OF CARD

In front of us stands the goat-headed representation of evil, the baphomet. On his head he wears a reversed Pentagram, which shows the domination or imprisonment of spirit by matter.

The use of the symbol of the goat's head as a symbol of evil stems from the biblical tradition of sending out a goat into the desert, symbolically laden with the sins of the community, as a way of propitiating the anger of God. Hence, the term 'scapegoat'.

THE DEVIL SPEAKS

'It is not often that I get the right of reply to any of the criticisms which are made against me. There are many that claim to know me, but when they point to the things in others which they think show me, they see only those aspects of themselves they cannot accept. One of my titles is "accuser", and this is what I do best when I assume the mantle of righteousness and point my finger at others. A classic example of this you can see when I appear as an outraged social worker or some other "authority" figure, hiding behind the false cloak of respectability. Be absolutely certain that when you hear someone pointing the finger at "the Devil's work", I am that person who is pointing the finger at another.

My purpose here in this world is to challenge you to become strong enough to oppose me. A long way back in time I was thrown out of heaven because I would not bow down to Adam, who had just had his first breath of air blown into him by the Most

High. Now I stand here in your path, blocking it, waiting for you to grow strong enough to throw me out of the way. But before you are able to live without me, you have a lot of growing to do first.'

ASTROLOGICAL ASSOCIATION

Capricorn – cardinal sign of Earth. Success, achievements.

DIVINATORY MEANING

The need to develop a more positive self-image. Don't over-emphasize the problems you are faced with: look upon them as opportunities for growth. Maintain your faith and keep alive your spirit of hope.

BULLET MEANING

Don't let your own negativity hold you back. Look at where you are setting yourself up for sabotage.

WORLDLY ASSOCIATIONS

Religious orthodoxy as a block to feelings. Sexual problems, feelings of inadequacy. Lack of vision. Feeling enslaved to a lifestyle that you are desperately unhappy with, but afraid to change. The fear of censure.

POSITIVE QUALITIES

Tough challenges. Climb every mountain – the view is great when you get to the top! Determination.

NEGATIVE QUALITIES

Feeling ignored. Love becomes irrelevant. Marriage for money/position/fame/power. Despair. Helplessness. Nobody hears me/nowhere to go.

----------------------- 16 THE TOWER -----------------------
DESCRIPTION OF CARD

A great tower stands against the horizon, being blasted by the elements, but, in particular, by lightning. Against this force, it begins to break apart, and as it does so, people begin to fall from the crumbling edifice into the waves below.

THE TOWER SPEAKS

'I am the Tower, and a symbol of all that is built upon the shifting sands of corruption and repression. For anything that is real or lasting, it must be established on a solid spiritual foundation. So much in your civilization is based on illusory values, and so the historical process repeats itself again and again so that what is built up collapses.

By the same token I represent the indomitable quality of the human spirit to rebuild, again and again, after calamity, wars and disasters. So, although nature may sweep our cities under the ocean, or break them with earthquakes and volcanoes, constantly we arise again and rebuild.'

ASTROLOGICAL ASSOCIATION

Mars – planet of energy, action, and power.

DIVINATORY MEANING

Having one's efforts overturned by external influences. The very real need to avoid accrediting the destructive process to 'the will of God' and take responsibility to prevent such ruin occurring again. Learn from the past.

BULLET MEANING

The need to build on solid foundations.

WORLDLY ASSOCIATIONS

Buildings, cities, civilisations. Armies, martial arts. Blacksmiths.

POSITIVE QUALITIES

The chance to rebuild in a better way. Necessary surgery.

NEGATIVE QUALITIES

Unnecessary destruction. Vandalism. Hooliganism. Needless violence. Fear on the streets.

17 THE STAR

DESCRIPTION OF CARD

A young maiden kneels naked by the side of a small stream, pouring water from two jars, one onto the earth, the other into the water itself. Behind her stand two trees; one is the Tree of Knowledge, the other is the Tree of Life. Above her we see the night sky, with blazing stars shining down.

THE STAR SPEAKS

'I am the Star of Hope and I am a symbol of that hope which is there after the troubles of the Tower experience have been dealt with.

As you can see from this beautiful garden which I inhabit, all around me are conditions of peace and tranquillity. Above my head shine the stars. They represent where we are headed on our long-term evolution. It could be quite a journey, don't you think? Who knows what adventures await us out there?'

ASTROLOGICAL ASSOCIATION

Aquarius – fixed sign of Air. Humanitarian.

DIVINATORY MEANING

The Star in a spread normally shows that powers which have been hidden until now will begin to show themselves. Thus, vital new energies begin to enter in on the equation. New encouragement, new motivation. Help 'from above'.

BULLET MEANING

Peace, serenity, tranquillity.

WORLDLY ASSOCIATIONS

Humanitarian endeavours. Live Aid. Environmental preservation. Protection of endangered species. Equal rights.

POSITIVE QUALITIES

The banning of cruel sports. International brother/sisterhood. Equal rights. Abolition of torture and vivisection.

NEGATIVE QUALITIES

Pious talking. Detached attitude. Emotionally cold.

---

18 THE MOON

DESCRIPTION OF CARD

We stand on an open road which runs between two towers. On one side stands a dog; on the other, a wolf. From the pool of water before us we see a lobster emerging, a symbol of the first stages of evolution.

Above in the sky, a full Moon can be seen rising.

THE MOON SPEAKS

'I am the Moon, Queen of the Night Sky.

When I am in the sky, most creatures are asleep. Thus I rule over their dreams, their fantasies, their nocturnal fears. I represent the instincts of all living creatures. I am the mother, triggering off all kinds of influences as I continue in my orbit around the Earth through the Zodiac. The scene that you see by my light is illuminated by reflected light, taken from the sun. Only your intuition, presentiment and inspiration will prove reliable for seeing through illusions, to spot deceptions and cut through delusions.'

ASTROLOGICAL ASSOCIATION

Pisces – mutable sign of Water. Receptivity.

DIVINATORY MEANING

The Moon card can suggest errors, self-deceptions, as well as the unexpected suddenly surfacing along the road of life. The real need to be very practical in all of your plans. The real possibility that you are living in a dream world. Check your dreams; they could well have some important message for you.

BULLET MEANING

Keep your feet on the ground. Don't let your emotions or imagination run away with you.

WORLDLY ASSOCIATION

Dreams, psychic tuning-in. Sensitive. Mirrors. Reflectors.

POSITIVE QUALITIES

Insightful. Memories.

NEGATIVE QUALITIES

Fears, phobias. Obsessions. Repeat patterns. Addictions.

---

19 THE SUN

DESCRIPTION OF CARD

In the garden we see a pair of twins playing. Above in the sky the sun is shining brightly.

Around the perimeter of the garden we see a wall, suggestive of the need for protection which the young twins have.

THE SUN SPEAKS

'I am the Sun and I am the centre of your universe. I am the provider of all light, heat, fuel, even indirectly, because even the coal and petroleum from your ground has been fathered by me.

Every morning, when I appear on your eastern horizon, I dispel the darkness and bring you effectively back to life.

When I am in your sky, you know that it is a time for action, for doing things. In the daylight you can see how things actually are, without your imagination running riot all the time. I shine upon each of you as my children, without favour for any. Yet, because of the shape of your world, some of you may not see me for long periods of time in the winter or may get scorched in your summer as a result of too much close proximity. Keeping you alive is a careful balance of too much and not enough of my presence.'

ASTROLOGICAL ASSOCIATION

The Sun – growth, the father.

DIVINATORY MEANING

An opportunity to plan, build, execute projects. Entering a period of sustained empowerment. Light after darkness.

BULLET MEANING

Growth and harmonious development of all areas of life.

WORLDLY ASSOCIATIONS

Gold. Aztecs. Pyramids. Architects' plans.

POSITIVE QUALITIES

Construction, doing. Openness. Accessibility.

NEGATIVE QUALITIES

Deserts. Drought. Intensity. Overbearing.

---

20 JUDGEMENT

DESCRIPTION OF CARD

A herald is coming out of the sky, blowing his horn and announcing the time for the seal of the earth to be opened, so that the dead can rise. A man, woman and child rise from their tomb of darkness to the light of a new life.

JUDGEMENT SPEAKS

'I am the final transformation you must pass through before you are ready to arrive at your destination. Through me you are able to shed the last considerations that tie you to the lower worlds of existence. I represent your passage through the underworld and the tremendous pressure which you have had to undergo through having had a material body. Now you have been purified to a higher state than you were before, just like diamonds emerging from coal having been under immense pressure for thousands – millions – of years.'

ASTROLOGICAL ASSOCIATION

Pluto – planet of transformation. Also the element of Fire.

DIVINATORY MEANING

Major transformative influences at work. The end of unpleasant times – relief from suffering or some tremendous pressure.

BULLET MEANING

Major transformation, possibly emigration.

WORLDLY ASSOCIATIONS

Black into white and vice versa. Molten lava. Hades, Lord of the Underworld.

POSITIVE QUALITIES

See the light. Change of heart. Conversion experience. Purification.

NEGATIVE QUALITIES

Fanaticism. Obsession. Narrow focus. Righteousness. Intolerance.

21 THE WORLD

DESCRIPTION OF CARD

A beautiful woman dances in the centre of a circle, surrounded by figures representing the four elements. In each hand she holds a rod or wand, symbolizing her mastery over the creative powers of life itself. In some representations she is encircled by a great serpent, which in biting its own tail represents the eternal cycle in all its perfection.

THE WORLD SPEAKS

'I am the World and in standing here I represent the fact that the integration of all of your essential components has been attained. When you get to this point, you will know how you can be in the world, but not necessarily tied down to purely worldly considerations.

Around me you see the emblems of the four elements, the man or anger for Air; the Lion for Fire; the Bull for Earth; and the Eagle to represent the higher aspect of Scorpio, which is our sign for Water. I am now at mastery over each of the elements, in other words, thoughts, emotions, actions and activities. I am no longer subject to the limitations which those things have placed on my life; similarly, if you are able to integrate the teachings throughout each of the proceeding Arcana, so will you be also.'

ASTROLOGICAL ASSOCIATION

Saturn – planet of lessons, teaching, responsibilities.

DIVINATORY MEANING

A very successful period is opening up for you. The achievement of an important objective in your life. Aim still higher, because the higher you aim the better. Dealing with the building blocks of reality. Entering a period of completing a karmic debt.

BULLET MEANING

Success, but the need for greater self-confidence.

WORLDLY ASSOCIATIONS

Scaffolding. Spirals. Pillars. A victory wreath.

POSITIVE ASSOCIATIONS

Responsibilities. Agriculture. The four seasons. Reliability. Trust.

NEGATIVE ASSOCIATIONS

Slow-moving. Pessimistic. Bitter. Gloomy.

MINOR ARCANA
THE SUIT OF COINS OR PENTACLES

This suit relates to material conditions of life; to those things which we can have, possess. It describes economic realities, and shows them as conditions of possibility, actuality and flux.

ACE

A new doorway opening up for exploration, which may well be beneficial to go through and explore. In particular it refers to work opportunity.

TWO

The same kind of work, but movement is shown here onto or into something else. More of a sideways transition. Often shows as a transfer of one kind or another.

THREE

The card for studying, for learning new subjects or enhancing existing skills, especially through training.

FOUR

Gathering coins together. The figure on the card is shown holding tightly onto a set of coins. Also, a single coin rests on his head, suggesting that money matters now dominate his thinking totally.

FIVE

Shows unforeseen expenses. A very dismal picture of poverty and also charity is given here. Again, as with other cards, it may not show what is, but rather give a warning as to what could be, unless steps are taken to avert it.

SIX

Rewarding on the basis of merit.

Sharing is the theme here. But how do we go about rewarding fairly? This card would also look at how we choose to share our time and energy, with others, between ourselves as individuals and our family, and so on.

SEVEN

Hard work, but approaching the harvest time. Notice how in this card we are only approaching our harvest time, i.e. a point where we can witness all of our efforts paying off and materializing. The figure in the card shows someone working with a hoe, not a scythe or other cutting instrument. The hoe is used for making water channels through which the plants can receive water. As he stares at the ripening crop, we become aware that it is still not yet ready to be plucked. As you can see, some of the Pentacles are still very small on the plants.

EIGHT

Skills properly applied.

This card is similar in some ways to the Three, in that it shows the same working tools being applied. Only here we have them being utilised in a far more professional manner than in the Three, where the figure was just beginning to get to grips with them. From the face of the man, we see that he now has a beard, showing maturity, while in the background he has amassed a small stock-pile of Pentacles which he has displayed on the wall behind him.

NINE

Gaining recognition, in one's own and others' estimation. The figure here stands dressed with a beautiful set of medallions around their chest. Reminiscent of the golden medallions awarded to athletes at Olympic competitions, it suggests the achievement of honours or recognition as the direct result of the individual's own efforts and abilities.

TEN

In some decks a family setting is shown, in others a man and a woman standing together, surrounded by a host of Pentacles. Either way it points towards a very stable material basis, upon which a long-term future can now be built. In particular it points towards joint finances, and important investment decisions.

PAGE

A young sergeant-at-arms stands looking out at the horizon. Represents looking around at one's own economic horizon for something new to get into. An alternative meaning is the preparedness to take on new responsibilities, as the young sergeant gets ready to become an officer.

KNIGHT

As with any of the Court cards, it can be taken to represent either a person or a process.

If it represents a person it shows a male figure that may be the Querent, or someone they are closely associated with in a work or economic capacity, who wishes to develop their work potential. They may be unsure of how to do that, or have definite ideas, but this can be explored in detail in the reading.

In the event of the card representing a process, it shows con-siderable action, getting things done. Knights, in medieval stories, would always be rushing around putting into effect the plans of their Kings and Queens.

QUEEN

If a person, then it shows the Querent or a woman they are closely associated with, work-wise or economically. Looking at the surrounding cards will give an idea of how positive or problematical that may seem.

If this represents a process, it shows more of relative condition of mastery over the economic forces of life.

KING

If a person, it shows the Querent or a man they are closely associated with economically.

Again, the surrounding cards will give an idea as to the viability.

If it represents a process, it indicates a period of economic strength.

——— THE SUIT OF SWORDS ———

The suit of Swords shows different kinds of conflict, their origins, how they might be averted and the characters involved. It shows also different states of mind which we can find ourselves in, especially when we are at odds or in conflict with our own or others' desires.

ACE

Breakthrough. We have here the upraised sword, emblematic of victory. We are reminded of all of the legends to do with swords, such as King Arthur and Excalibur, Siegfried, etc. The cutting of the ties that bind.

TWO

The figure in the card sits blindfolded with two swords in her lap, each pointing in a different direction. Indecision.

THREE

A human heart pierced by three swords. Heartbreak, unless you can communicate.

FOUR

The lifting of tensions. A young knight rests on the ground while above him we see three swords being lifted away. Beside him lays another sword, which is his.

FIVE

Crossed swords. A parting of the ways is shown here. Two people part company, while a third picks up the swords which they have thrown aside.

SIX

Sailing away from negativity. In crossing the great dividing water, the people shown in the boat have basically said, 'We've had enough, let's move on and find something else.'

SEVEN

The need for vigilance. Also, an important but worthwhile sacrifice being made. A rather shadowy figure creeps into our encampment and makes off with five swords, leaving behind two that presumably he cannot carry.

EIGHT

Frustration. The need for patience. If the woman struggles against the limiting power of the swords, i.e. her situation, at this time, then she will only succeed in hurting herself. Here, she must exercise self-control and wait until a change takes place in her situation before she dissipates any further energy in trying to set herself free.

NINE

Isolation – the need to open up new channels of communication with others as a way of breaking out of this.

TEN

Major changes – not always ones that are desired – but the negative aspect of these can be minimized or even completely reversed by going along with them and in that way turning them to your advantage.

PAGE

The figure shows a young, inexperienced boy about to rush into a situation of conflict, armed with only a toy sword. The most he can achieve is that of getting himself into trouble. Don't rush into battle – and don't rush into other peoples' battles either!

KNIGHT

If this represents a person, it shows the Querent or a man that they are closely associated with in a conflict situation. The Knight may be on their side or an adversary. This card can sometimes suggest the use of conciliation and negotiation rather than the continuation of hostilities.

If it represents a process, it points to the need to prepare for battle, the kind of battle being suggested by the surrounding cards.

QUEEN

This could represent either the Querent or a woman which they are associated with in a scene of conflict.

It could also represent a process, showing what needs to be mastered in order to swing the balance of power more in the Querent's favour.

KING

If this card represents a person, it shows the Querent or a man whom they are associated with, in a situation of having won a great victory. By looking at the surrounding cards, we would be able to tell the nature of that victory and whether it has worked out to the Querent's advantage or otherwise.

If it represents a process or an event, it suggests that you do not have to continue struggling. Rather, it might show that the right time has come to reassess whether or not the time is right for consolidation. In other words, for taking benefit of the gains already achieved.

THE SUIT OF WANDS

The suit of Wands shows us states of energy, action and power. Mobility and doing things are the qualities referred to here.

ACE

A new enterprise being started. By looking at the surrounding cards we would have an idea as to what.

TWO

Good advice being given and received. In the card we see two figures talking closely together, as if secrets were being shared or important guidance asked for.

In one hand we see a crystal ball, which we take as having been used for scrying purposes.

THREE

Shows a figure looking down from a hill top, surveying the scene with an experienced eye. Leading others by example.

FOUR

Welcome home! The poles are dressed for an important guest to return to the castle and that guest is to be greatly honoured. Working with other people toward a common purpose.

FIVE

Conflict. Stiff competition. Push through this with very strong determination.

SIX

Victory; the time being shown here in which you enter into the city amid great fanfare, after having overcome a strong, opposing force.

SEVEN

Cut down your problems one by one. Don't let them build up and overwhelm you. In this card you see someone who is trying to take on everything all at once. Not always the best way to secure victory.

EIGHT

Here we see a set of 'flying wands' crossing high up over land and sea.

The person's life is speeding up. Possible travel opportunities.

NINE

Allow other people to support you in your undertakings: you don't have to be so defensive.

TEN

Don't carry everyone else's burdens and problems. It's time to put them down and let other people begin to take responsibility for their own lives.

PAGE

Learning and/or travel is shown here, as the Page prepares himself for a journey which will take him through foreign lands, suggested by the mountains/pyramids shown behind him in the distance.

KNIGHT

Dynamic male energy. If it represents a person, it would show the Querent or someone with whom they are connected in some area of activity.

If it represents a process, it indicates the need for a high level of energy in order to handle the tasks at hand.

QUEEN

If it represents a person, it shows either the Querent or someone they are connected with as an independent-minded woman.

If it represents a process it shows mastery over the level of action required by the situation. Initiative.

KING

If it represents a person, it shows either the Querent or someone that they are connected with as a man of leadership.

If it represents a process it shows that the situation would require the initiative of the Querent.

───────────────── THE SUIT OF CUPS ─────────────────

The suit of Cups represents the element Water, which stands for emotions, feelings.

ACE

Emotional fulfilment. Here we see a cup which 'runneth over'.

TWO

Either a new relationship starting or a new phase of an existing relationship.

THREE

Reunions, celebrations. If one isn't being planned, then this card might well suggest that it should be.

FOUR

The need to reach out for new friendships. In this card, the figure sits under a tree, looking into the cups – or friendships and relationships which they represent – but is failing to notice that another cup is being offered from out of the blue. This fourth cup, this unexpected offer of friendship or love, could well be what the figure is looking for.

FIVE

Disillusionment, if you rely on the commitments of others. The need for self-reliance. Also, don't focus so much on the past. Here, the figure in the card must turn around from what has been spilled and drink afresh from the cups which stand upright.

SIX

Learning to give and receive on an emotional level.

Two people face each other, each offering the other a cup of friendship, from which flowers are growing. This card is similar to the Two of Cups, but here, there is a sense of something – shown by the flowers – having already grown, rather than something starting completely afresh.

SEVEN

Confusion – the need to get your own priorities in order.

In this card, the figure stands looking through the mists of confusion at all of the different possibilities which life is showing them. From one cup we see a house, representing security; from another jewels for wealth. From a third we see a snake, symbolizing sexuality, while from another we see a Dragon, for wisdom. In the other cups we have a human face, for relationships, a wreath for fame and a mask for self-identity.

The Querent must choose which of these items is the most important.

EIGHT

Looking for something on a much deeper level. The figure in the card has stacked up all of the cups in their life, but has found that there is something important missing. So important is it for this person to find that missing cup, that they have donned a cloak and are now walking along the lonely road to go in search of it.

NINE

Experiencing life as a celebration.

The figure in this card is clearly at the centre of a celebration, rejoicing their good fortune. If, in the Querent's life, there is little for them to be happy about, then this card would encourage them to look for things – small things maybe – over which they can begin to count themselves lucky.

TEN

Emotional commitments. A man and a woman stand arm in arm, and feel themselves to have arrived at a point where they can stand and take stock of what they have created for themselves for their own happiness. This card is not predicting marriage, but instead is getting the Querent to look at what it is that they want from their loving relationships; what commitments do they intend to make and which ones to keep? How do they go about choosing someone as a partner? Should they be more choosy and expect more or are they content to take 'second best'?

PAGE

If it represents a situation, it shows new contacts, particularly socially.

If it represents a person, it shows someone in the process of learning more about themselves, their feelings, hopes and aspirations. It can also show someone not yet confident about themselves.

KNIGHT

This card shows an individual or a situation involving an individual in which strong emotions are involved. The person could be a lover, a friend or a symbol of how the Querent is interacting with others emotionally. In a man's cards, it would show either him or a friend; in a woman's cards, it would generally show a man in her life, or the 'male' (active) side of her personality.

QUEEN

In a woman's cards, it would generally show either her, or a woman significant in her life in an emotional sense. In a man's cards, it would show either a significant woman or the 'female' (receptive) side of his personality.

KING

This card generally shows not so much a person as a situation of culmination. Thus, a certain emotional scenario has been resolved; a state of happiness is either achieved or achievable. This card portrays a man with a calm ocean behind him. The ocean represents the realm of feelings, which are now becalmed.

9

SPREADS AND
LAYOUTS

In working out how the individual cards may link together the main thing to remember is that you are not necessarily going to come out with something astonishingly 'psychic' – at least not at first. When you have become more experienced in the 'art' of reading, then things will slot together a lot more smoothly.

Try to get a mental picture of what is going on in the life of the person in front of you. You will do this a number of times with lesser and greater degrees of success. Don't be too hard on yourself at this point if it's not all sweetness and light. Later on you will be able to flit from one card to another with apparent ease, effortlessly linking them together as you go.

Stay calm and relaxed; if it doesn't seem to be working at first have patience. In our society, we have become so used to the notion of things being instant: instant coffee, instant success, instant love. The ancient mysteries reveal themselves only to those who truly desire to know them. So it is not unreasonable to suppose that in some way, your sincerity of intention to learn the Tarot is being put to the test at this point.

At first you can use a Teddy bear or a doll in front of you – just to get you used to having 'someone' in front of you as you start to read the cards. Also, it is important to verbalize what you are seeing there in the cards.

Don't worry about sounding silly or anything like that. You are going through the same experience of self-consciousness as someone learning how to sing or act, or learning a musical instrument for the first time. So you are not necessarily going to sound like Pavarotti; even he probably didn't sound like much when he first started.

You will find it useful to have a set of friends round for an evening's Tarot party, just to give yourself the confidence to start reading other people's cards.

You may feel nervous about asking a complete stranger if you can read their cards: but what better opportunity to confront your fears than by doing so? You could even start off in the launderette or in your local pub, if you feel up to it.

You could simply place your Tarot deck on the table and let the person next to you pick them up and ask you about the cards. Tell them that you are on a Tarot course and ask if they wouldn't mind being a guinea pig for about half an hour or so. And you would almost certainly find people who would derive benefit from the reading experience. Wherever you go, you will meet people who need the insights, the knowledge and understanding which can come from the reading which you can give them.

Don't worry too much about fancy-shaped spreads, which can become so complex they actually prevent the truth from filtering down into the reading. Instead, use the technique of actually laying out further cards on top of the card you require further information from. Remember that you can use this on any card that you want to go into further detail with.

Remember that this enhancing technique works on the basis of 'The moment the question is asked (or thought of) = the moment the answer is given.'

So when you want to go into more detail, just lay out, say, three or four extra cards on top of the area you are looking into, and regard those symbols as pertaining to the question or the area being 'opened up'.

One question in your mind is 'How many cards should I lay out on top of the original?' and the answer to this is really whatever seems right to you at the time. Try to avoid the temptation to lay out dozens of extra cards, because this will only confuse things. But if you lay out just one or two, you might not have enough scope for your imagination to work with.

As an alternative to this, you might feel more comfortable in getting the Querent to actually pick out two or three more cards in association with each question and lay them out adjacent to that area on their spread which pertains most symbolically to their question.

Here is a sample reading using the enhancing technique:

'The Lovers card shows that the issue which is most clearly in your thoughts at this time is relationships. By itself it doesn't necessarily show that you are involved with someone, but it does indicate that when you are, the involvement is very intense. Let's have a look at this area and see what else is there ...'

Here, three (for example) cards are laid down, either directly from the top of the deck or as selected by the Querent. As synchronicity would have it, we have these cards:

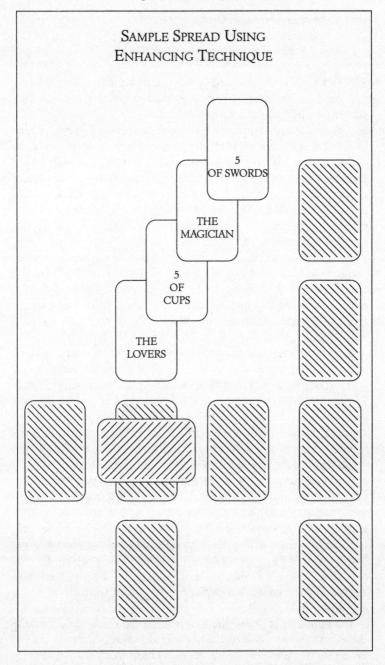

SAMPLE SPREAD USING
ENHANCING TECHNIQUE

5
OF SWORDS

THE
MAGICIAN

5
OF
CUPS

THE
LOVERS

Five of Cups: Disillusionment
The Magician: Communicating to others
Five of Swords: Break-up between people

Now that we have the trail of enhancing cards laid out, let's try and see how an imaginative interpretation of these complementary cards might come together.

'These cards are emphasizing a tendency in your previous relationships to become very *disillusioned* when *breakups* have occurred: this may be due to insufficient *communication* between you and a partner at the outset of a relationship as to your mutual expectations. If it is you that wants *commitment*, you would need to put this across to the other person right from the start and to be clear about the kind of *signals* you are giving out.'

From here, you would elaborate.

As you read through the cards in a Querent's spread, let them come to life by recalling the results you achieved in doing the Worksheets, which brought to mind all your own past experiences, thoughts, hopes and anxieties. Bring these experiences into the reading which you are doing with this enhancing technique.

Later on in your journey you can get into fancy spreads, but let's get you literate before you try tackling Shakespeare's Sonnets.

As you progress, you will increasingly come to the point of 'getting a sense of perspective' of a spread of cards. As this happens, you will not feel the need to go through the cards so systematically, but you will be able to leap about, picking at cards from different areas of the spread and fusing them in ways which you haven't done before, or even previously considered.

As you continue in your journey, the cards will begin to shift in their original meaning, and to take on other associations, or to assume other meanings and attributions. You see, you haven't learnt something which is static – your relationship with the Tarot is going to be something which undergoes constant change – just like a relationship with a friend or lover. So don't expect the meanings – or even your readership style – to remain fixed and unchanging. Instead, be aware of *how* it is growing and in *what way* it is evolving.

You may find at times that in a reading the cards are indicating the exact opposite of what has occurred in the Querent's life. For example, the Empress in the past position does not necessarily indicate that the Querent has experienced a sense of his or her artistic capability growing. The Querent might even say that the exact opposite occurred. In this case, the Tarot is actually asking you to get your Querent to take a look at what happened in the past that prevented it from happening.

The Tarot reveals areas in a person's life where things are going on – or where things aren't going on, *but should be*. It will raise relevant issues which need to be looked at by the individual receiving the reading, rather than definitively describing everything that is going on with accuracy. Where this notion came from that a Tarot reading has to be 'accurate', I don't know. To my mind, it is like saying that a painting has to be accurate. A photograph should be accurate, but not a painting. I mean, were Leonardo's paintings 'accurate'? Was Van Gogh's work 'accurate'? Just as the nineteenth century insisted that all new ideas were compatible with Christianity, so the twentieth century insists upon compatibility with scientific method or 'accuracy'.

So if a reading seems to be showing the opposite to what is occurring in the Querent's life, then don't forget that it is revealing blockages and barriers which are preventing the realization of their full potential.

Here you can bring in the Tarot counselling process of asking relevant and open-ended questions to enable your Querent to 'take a look' at what might be the underlying causes of their being blocked, and, hopefully, in identifying them, to be able to map out a new course of direction so as to rise above them.

The question has often been raised as to whether you should read for a Querent in front of a third person, e.g. a girlfriend or family member. You might find that the Querent is able to open up a lot more easily if the two of you are alone than if they have someone else sitting there observing everything.

In the following pages we are including other possible spreads. Try them out, because different spreads work for different people in different situations. It is important not to get too limited by following only one pattern or style. It's actually something that can happen all too easily.

Some people have found that the traditional Celtic Cross is a bit unwieldy. What you might like to try before going straight on to this is Triadic Spread. The Triad – or Three Rays of Light – was a symbol of the ancient Druids, in particular, of the Chosen Chief of the Order. That aside, for one reason or another, a lot of people I have trained have found it a lot easier to get started on this one. In a nutshell, one line is to show the past, the middle shows the present and the other line shows the future possibilities. As you lay out the cards in this pattern, you can add to them with cards off the top of the deck which your Querent has shuffled. It just keeps opening up the person's life. There isn't any fixed number of cards which you have to lay out; as many as you feel appropriate to the situation. Let yourself be the judge as to what works or doesn't work.

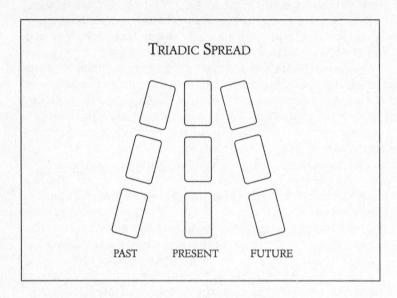

TRIADIC SPREAD

PAST   PRESENT   FUTURE

In time, when you are more confident, you can feel free to do without formal spreads if you so desire. Or you could create your own, assigning to your spread whatever meaning you want for the duration of that spread. In future spreads you can again reassign meaning and significance. Remember that there is ultimately no one true meaning to any card placement. It was only another human being sitting there with pen in hand which said that it was.

When you are asked a question by the Querent in the course of a reading, bear in mind that you can at that point interpret all of the cards in the spread from the point of view of answering that particular question. And when you are asked another question, you can reassign the meaning of the cards in front of you and take them as referring to *that* question. So, even when you are asked many questions, you can keep the same spread of cards on the table but just flit from vantage point to vantage point and use the same set of symbols with which to answer each of the different questions.

One question you will ask is how is it possible to get dates and timings on events in the future or how to be specific about places, countries, etc. When you are asked a question that requires you to be specific, let your mind go completely blank for a moment, and 'allow' the answer to come to you. For example, if asked 'When will XYZ happen?', allow yourself to go into your quiet centre, and let the figure come to you. If you don't get any number or picture, fine, don't force it. But the way of getting yourself to use your native intuitive muscles is by starting to flex them. You are not going to be right 100 per cent of the time. I'm not always 100 per cent right. But when someone asks me to be specific I use this technique, and more often than not I'm right in what I am able to predict. If I don't get any number or picture, I don't force it. I only ever pass on to others what I'm picking up on. So don't let yourself be psychologically pushed into coming up with something you honestly can't access into. You will not be completely right or 'accurate' either. But you can be completely honest to yourself and your Querent.

Some people have said that you can get an idea of when something is going to happen by looking at the number which is on a relevant card: e.g. the Six of Cups would indicate love in six days, weeks, months, etc. I personally don't go for this – I have never found it to be a reliable guideline.

SPREADS

Spreads are just formations of cards which have become traditionally used amongst Tarot readers over time. *It is perfectly possible to create your own spread* – there is nothing sacrosanct about any particular formation or any of their variants, such as the Celtic Cross. You will come across some sources which dogmatically state that the cards must be placed in a certain pattern; I have never found that it makes much difference. What is important is that once you have created a pattern and assigned value to the card placements, you don't constantly change them around at whim.

Why is it called the Celtic Cross? The Celtic Cross is a symbol of life's renewal and the Cross is made out of cards 1 to 6. The cards from 7 to 10 form a pillar which stands to the right of the High Priestess in the Temple of Solomon. Some would attribute significance to these shapes, but their employment in readings doesn't necessarily give any more insight than any other kind of spread.

When your Querent has finished shuffling the cards, take them back and lay them out in the pattern suggested.

THE CELTIC CROSS

1. The general situation
2. The general situation
3. On your mind
4. The influences of the last three years (background influences)
5. Recent influences
6. The influences of the coming year
7. Doorway from the present to the future
8. Domestic life
9. Hopes or anxieties
10. The overview/any other business

The first two cards are taken together and show the mingling of influences which are at work in the Querent's life at present. The first card is the predominant influence, while the second is more the 'filter'; in other words, how it is going to show itself.

The third card shows what is on the Querent's mind, i.e. the way they are actually experiencing their current situation or the kind of thoughts that make up their consciousness.

The fourth and fifth cards give us something of a historical backdrop – the fourth showing more long-term influences, while the fifth shows more recent patterns or events.

The sixth card shows the kind of influences which the Querent is shortly to move into, while the seventh tells us how that may be most effectively achieved. The seventh card is a kind of 'bridge' showing the steps which the Querent must take in order to make the reading actually 'work'.

The eighth card gives us an insight into the Querent's domestic life, their home and family scenario.

The ninth card opens a window to the Querent's hopes, or, if a 'negative' card comes up, some of their anxieties and apprehensions.

The tenth card is not so much a 'final outcome', as some of the introductory booklets would have it, but rather a *general overview* of the Querent's life. Here we may well also have 'any other business' not being looked at by any preceding card. It can be a bit of a mixed bag.

Here we have a very simple, easy to remember, but still very effective way of opening up a Querent's life.

THE FIFTEEN-CARD SPREAD

After shuffling, take the cards back and lay them out in three rows each of five cards (see page 161). The first will give you an outline of their past, the second will tell you about their present, while the third row will indicate how they are to move ahead.

THE ASTROLOGICAL OR CIRCLE SPREAD

This spread (see page 162) is based around the astrological 12 houses which are to be found in any natal or birth chart. Each card placement is linked to the meaning of the 'house' or section of the circle and moves anti-clockwise – as tradition has it – round in a circle.

The first card is laid out in the 9 o'clock position. This card represents the personality influences of the Querent: who they are, their basic characteristics, their approach to life.

The second card gives the reader an idea of the Querent's sense of value: what is 'precious' to them, where their 'wealth' lies. For some, this will be in purely material considerations, whereas for others, other senses of value will be shown (e.g. friendships, children, peace of mind).

The third card shows us how they communicate with others and how they receive communication. Study influences, as well as the influence of brothers and sisters (if any) can also come under this heading.

The fourth card tells us about the Querent's home life, both in the sense of their original home and that which they have created for themselves in present time. It can also at times show us the influence on their personality of their mother.

The fifth card gives us an insight into the Querent's love life, although we must not be too mechanistic about this: we could well get a lot of insight on this as well as other areas of the Querent's life from cards in other positions. Children, also, are in this domain, and can sometimes show their influence in this position.

The sixth card gives us information about the Querent's work life: their association with their colleagues; their association with their colleagues at work. Health, both physical and mental, is also at times indicated in this position.

The seventh card represents the Querent's love life, but in a slightly different sense from that of the fifth. Whereas the fifth is more the house of passion, the seventh is more to do with partnerships and relationships of more long-term commitment.

The eighth card is able to show us about the Querent's 'power', i.e. their ability to make significant changes in their lives or otherwise, as the case may be. It shows us if there are any powerful, transformative influences at work. Also in this category, we might find other people's resources which can be used to the Querent's benefit.

The ninth card is a window into the Querent's philosophy on life. Travel and learning – in fact anything which is mind-expanding – is shown here. Associations with individuals normally outside the Querent's own walk of life also come into this category.

The tenth card shows us what the Querent wants to achieve: how success is most likely to come to him and what success actually means. For different people, it can mean substantially different things.

The eleventh card gives the reader an insight into the Querent's social life, and tells us about friendships involvement with groups of people and societies on a wider level.

The twelfth and final card shows us about the Querent's spiritual

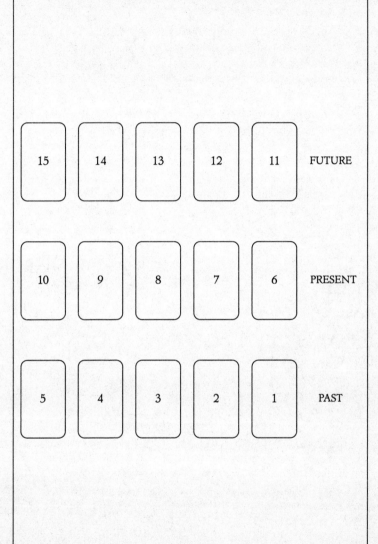

FIFTEEN-CARD SPREAD

| 15 | 14 | 13 | 12 | 11 | FUTURE |

| 10 | 9 | 8 | 7 | 6 | PRESENT |

| 5 | 4 | 3 | 2 | 1 | PAST |

THE ASTROLOGICAL OR CIRCLE SPREAD

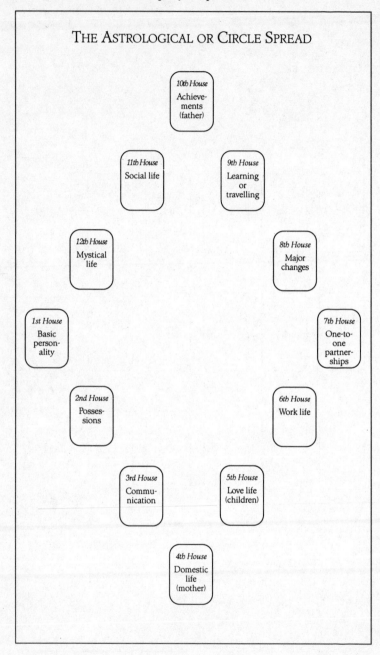

10th House
Achieve-
ments
(father)

11th House
Social life

9th House
Learning
or
travelling

12th House
Mystical
life

8th House
Major
changes

1st House
Basic
person-
ality

7th House
One-to-
one
partner-
ships

2nd House
Posses-
sions

6th House
Work life

3rd House
Commu-
nication

5th House
Love life
(children)

4th House
Domestic
life
(mother)

RELATIONSHIP SPREAD

The relationship from the Querents' point of view

1 Origins of the relationship	**2** Where it is coming from	**3** – Present – Where the relationship is now	**4** Where it is going	**5** How it ultimately evolves

The relationship from the other person's point of view

6 Origins of the relationship	**7** Where it is coming from	**8** – Present – Where the relationship is now	**9** Where it is going	**10** How it ultimately evolves

and mystical life – or absence of one! It may also show what they need to do in order to feel more complete as a person.

THE RELATIONSHIP SPREAD

Relationships fall into an area which many people will want to know a lot about. What you have here is a spread which specifically deals with that area (see above).

The cards are laid out in two rows. The upper row represents the relationship from the point of view of the Querent. The lower row represents the relationship from the point of view of the other person involved, who obviously will not be present when this spread is done. The Querent shuffles and hands the cards back to you. You then spread them out in the way shown in the diagram.

You will find this an astonishingly insightful process. Have fun! The Querent could write down the observations and discuss them with the partner or friend to whom the spread refers.

This spread can also be used to find out how others see you, the mistakes you have made (if any!), or at least to get an idea of what you could be doing to improve your situation.

CONSULTATION SHEETS

It is sometimes useful to write up what you see in each spread. I have provided a few examples for you to practise on. Remember, there is no right or wrong answer, only what you can see in the cards is relevant, so I have not provided any model readings.

If you find this a useful exercise, it may help you with actual readings if you keep a note of them in this form. So, according to the following situations, please write down your own interpretations.

EXAMPLE 1

A Querent wants to know about her ex-boyfriend. He keeps coming back to her. What are the problems? What does she need to do in order to improve her situation? Should she take him back or will she find a new relationship?

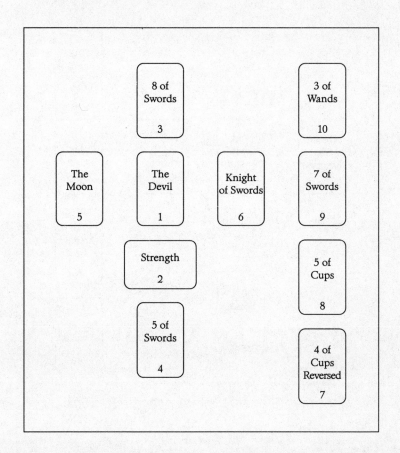

EXAMPLE 2

A Querent wants to know about their business. What are the problems? What do they need to do in order to improve the situation?

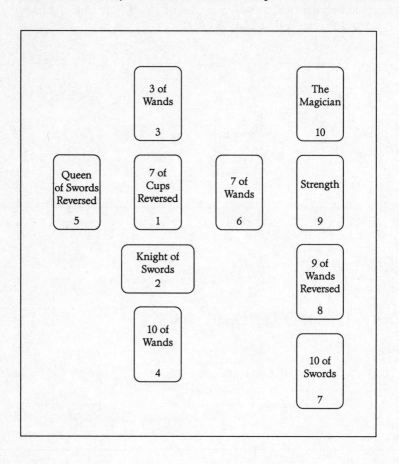

EXAMPLE 3

A Querent wants to know about a possible promotion. What are the possible obstacles? What should be done in order to get it?

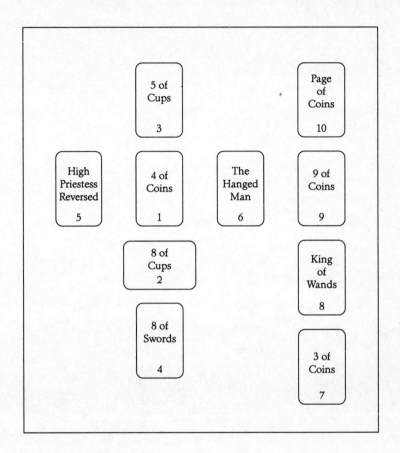

EXAMPLE 4

Write down your own interpretation of this astrological spread, as a general reading.

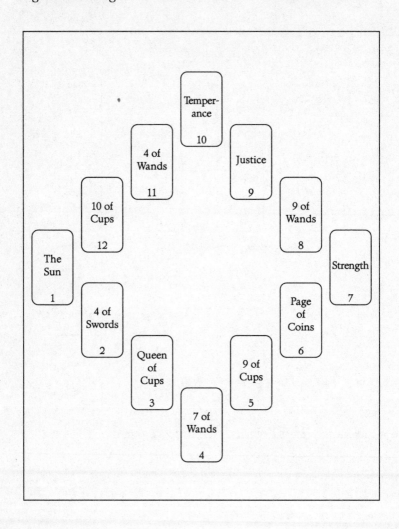

EXAMPLE 5

For each of these simple spreads, imagine a different Querent.
The Querent has been offered a new job. Should they take it, and
if so, how will it turn out?

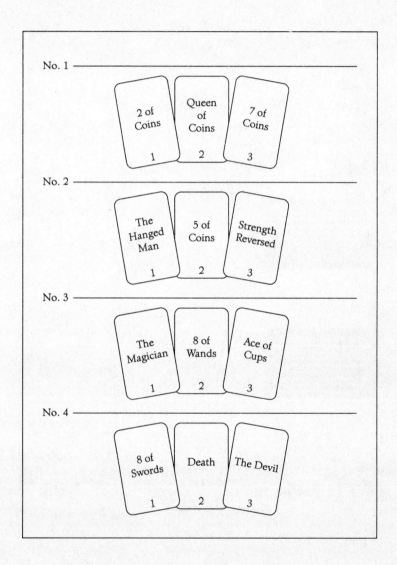

EXAMPLE 6

For each of these simple spreads, imagine a different Querent. The Querent has just started a new relationship. How will it work out?

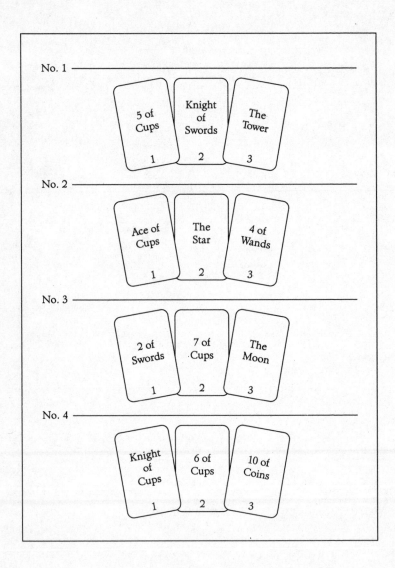

EXAMPLE 7

For each of these simple spreads, imagine a different Querent. The Querent is about to move house. How will it turn out?

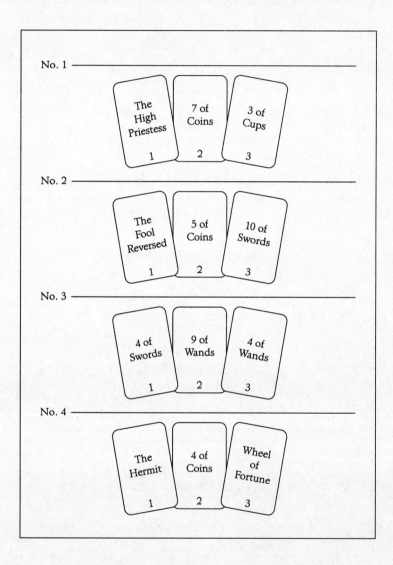

No. 1

The High Priestess	7 of Coins	3 of Cups
1	2	3

No. 2

The Fool Reversed	5 of Coins	10 of Swords
1	2	3

No. 3

4 of Swords	9 of Wands	4 of Wands
1	2	3

No. 4

The Hermit	4 of Coins	Wheel of Fortune
1	2	3

EXAMPLE 8

For each of these simple spreads, imagine a different Querent. The Querent wishes to know what spiritual paths they should follow.

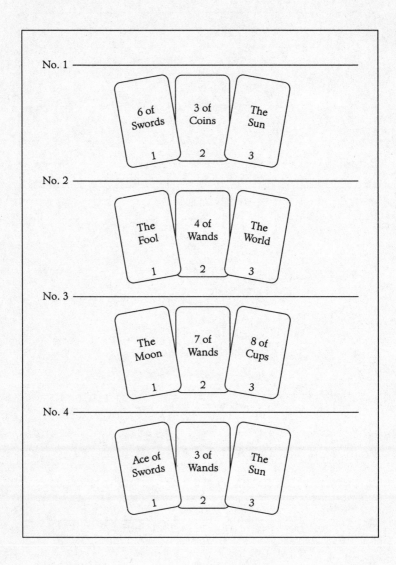

EXAMPLE 9

For each of these simple spreads, imagine a different Querent. The Querent wishes to know about their child's education. What might they be suggesting?

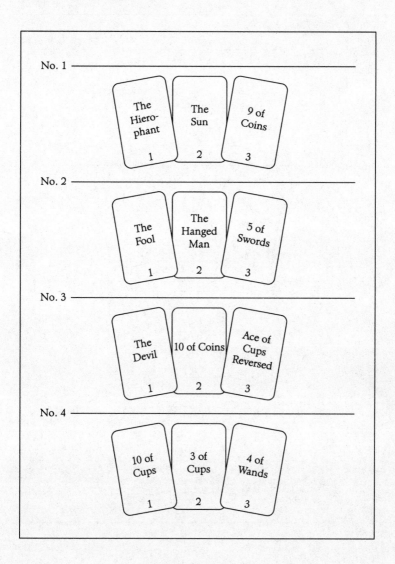

EXAMPLE 10

For each of these simple spreads, imagine a different Querent. The Querent wishes to know what might be their life's lessons.

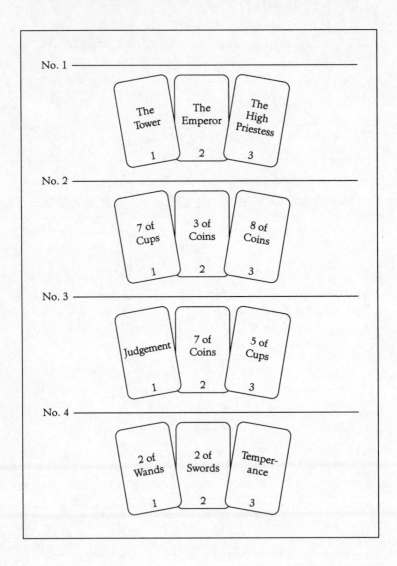

No. 1

| The Tower 1 | The Emperor 2 | The High Priestess 3 |

No. 2

| 7 of Cups 1 | 3 of Coins 2 | 8 of Coins 3 |

No. 3

| Judgement 1 | 7 of Coins 2 | 5 of Cups 3 |

No. 4

| 2 of Wands 1 | 2 of Swords 2 | Temperance 3 |

10

CARD REVERSALS

With regard to card reversals, when you see them there in the spread, don't get into negative or apocalyptic meanings. Don't start reversing the meanings of the cards mechanically. Here you must slowly but surely begin to use your own sense of direction.

There will be times when you feel that a card reversal will mitigate, increase or reduce the level of intensity of the card, or possibly even reverse an upright meaning. There will be times when you feel that it signifies a delay in the 'coming into being' of something. There will be times when you feel that it bears absolutely no significance.

Don't forget – it is your job to make the cards fit the Querent's life, not the other way round. Having said that, if you really feel that a card reversed has got something worthwhile to offer, then go right ahead and read it in the way which it is suggesting to you.

That is, after all, the whole philosophy of the Tarot: that we allow ourselves to be guided by our intuition – our own capacity to know what is right or real at any time, above and beyond any sense of knowing how we might know.

In general, don't pay too much attention to card reversals. After all, how much more mechanistic could you get? Even if a card came up reversed, it wouldn't necessarily mean that the Querent had reversed it. It might well have been turned upside down by the previous Querent.

A reversed card might well suggest the need to investigate further how a particular theme might apply or be looked at by the Querent. Particular cards come up not necessarily to describe what is taking place, but what needs to be avoided, or minimized, or emphasized.

There really is no hard and fast formula that can be given to prepare you for every possible eventuality, only that of reading a strange and unlikely combination of upright and reversed cards in a Querent's spread as a learning experience, as a chance to see how guidance can take place given the particular set of symbols which synchronicity has placed there. So it really is a question of finding your own way through.

The little instruction booklets which accompany every deck are sometimes full of references to 'a deceitful woman', or 'a capricious man', when they refer to card reversals. I believe that we should try to avoid as much as possible giving negative and disempowering interpretations to cards, especially when they refer to people in the Querent's life. A lot of people have been frightened by sensationalistic and thoughtless readers. Many people have been influenced by these experiences and need to have their fears allayed, to be shown that the Tarot is something that is 'safe'. There is enough negativity, fear and suspicion out there without us adding to it.

This is not to say that everything in life is sweetness and light. Far from it. But we are here to empower people who want to improve and develop their lives – not disempower them.

11
PRACTICAL TAROT GUIDELINES

1 DON'T BE TOO ANALYTICAL

There is a need to be extremely flexible in your interpretation of the Tarot in a reading. Your job is to find a way of making sense of what you see reflected in the Querent's cards. It is not to enforce a reality on them. Because a card is there it doesn't necessarily describe what is actually happening, but possibly describes what should be, or could have been, instead of what is. Don't try and work it all out in your head. Just because a particular card has come up in a spread you don't have to spend hours and hours trying to work out why. If you can't slot it together at first, move on to an area in the spread where you feel you can get down to work. You can always come back later on to the troublesome spot, if you want to at all.

2 DEALING WITH INVALIDATION

This follows on from the last point really. Only here the Querent isn't just unable to work out what their cards are referring to: they are refusing to look into their lives at all. You may well have touched upon areas which are too sensitive for them to have begun to approach, let alone share. The response which you will get from this sort of Querent is hostile.

With these guys it is best that you close the reading. It is preferable for you to withdraw from a reading with your dignity intact than to keep hacking away with a Querent who doesn't actually want to get anything from the experience. But I mention this as a last resort.

An intermediate option would be to ask the Querent what it is that they would like to get from the reading. And then to insist that they help you to try to find *how* the cards might apply.

3 GET THE ATTENTION OF THE QUERENT

Slow down the speed of your voice if you want to make a point more dramatic. This also has the advantage of giving you a bit more time in which to think about what you are going to say. Don't overdo it to the point that you start to lose your own natural style of self-expression, but allow yourself to be a bit more dramatic than you normally would. After all, you are delivering a Tarot reading, not just holding an ordinary conversation. Allow yourself to use hand movements that permit you to express more fully the message that is flowing through you. Create impact by all means, but don't go overboard or become overly dramatic.

4 IT'S NOT A BAD IDEA TO LAY THE CARDS OUT LOTS OF TIMES

Remember, number of times over material = certainty of results. If you run out of people to practise on, then get a Teddy bear or a doll and practise on that instead.

Some people have asked me: 'How many times should you allow yourself to flunk, before you should jack it in and forget about Tarot readership?'

The question is really an irrelevant one. It's the same as someone asking how many times should you allow a young baby to try to walk before you get bored and tired of its repeated failures and simply forbid it from ever trying to walk again! Well, here you obviously wouldn't forbid the child from trying to walk again. You'd make the child keep on trying until it got the hang of it and became able to walk. And whether that took just a few weeks, a few months, or even a few years isn't really the point.

Of course it would be nice for the baby to learn to walk properly in the shortest space of time possible. It would be nice to be able to learn how to read Tarot in just a few days – ideally. But life isn't necessarily like that. Some of us are in such a hurry to get to the other end of our training experience with the Tarot, so that we can have a sense of completion. But it's not necessary to rush it. It's not at all a bad thing to take your time and savour each of the subtleties of meaning. We should take time to allow ourselves to actually digest the powerful spiritual input of knowledge and wisdom which the Tarot contains.

There is a need for patience. All of us are guilty to some extent of living our lives too quickly. With the Tarot, we should slow down a bit and try to give each of our psychic and spiritual taste-buds the chance to savour what these fantastic symbols have to teach us.

It will open up to you when you follow through on your exercises.

5 CONCENTRATION WHILST SHUFFLING

It really seems to make quite a difference to an actual reading. You could get the Querent to breathe into the cards, for example! Or at the least to 'put their thoughts into the cards'. This way they are actually putting more of their own life energy into the deck, and there will be more synchronicity between the rhythm of their lives and the cards which fall out for them in a spread. Otherwise we are just going to have a completely random selection of cards which don't have any necessary connection to the Querent's life.

6 DON'T PANIC – DON'T DESPAIR

If you find that you can't make sense of all of the cards in front of you in a spread, don't panic and don't despair! When you first start doing readings, you will notice that the tension between yourself and your Querent is very considerable. The other person – not to mention yourself – is under a very great pressure of expectation. You are feeling very much centre stage, that you have 'to get it right' – and that if you don't or can't you are going to look like an absolute fool.

Just relax. Start the reading with a brief outline of some of the cards which 'stand out' more than the others. Just start talking and allow the Tarot to speak through you. It really will happen a lot more easily if you let this flow through and stop trying to 'make it happen right now'.

Don't expect too much. The message of the Tarot in *any* reading scenario is almost always simple, clear, measured. It is in this quality that we find truth. Too much intellectualization has more to do with the emptiness of modern philosophy than the truths which the Tarot cards point towards.

7 DON'T TRY TO FIT ALL THE CARDS INTO A SINGLE READING

You might, for instance, feel that the reading comes to a natural end after you have read only half of the cards in the person's spread. Don't feel pressurized to tell the Querent something which they want to hear, if you feel that it is not a part of the message which is intended for them in that reading. Be honest – and if you don't see something as being true or valid, then say so.

8 BE NIMBLE AND RESPONSIVE

Be nimble – responsive to what is being revealed in the reading through the Querent's body and facial language. After all, we are reading the entire person, not just what is being shown by the random sample of cards which have turned up in that spread. If we were reading their cards alone it would be possible to put a Tarot reading on a computer disk and let the computer pull cards at random.

Some people who know more about computers than about Tarot have actually done just that. But to me it has no meaning. Be aware of when what you are saying makes sense to the Querent – and when it doesn't. Remember – it is no invalidation of your skills if the reading at first doesn't seem to fit. Any bespoke tailor will ask his Querent back two or three times in order to get the best possible fitting of what he has made. Allow yourself the space and time to 'tailor-make' your reading of the cards to the person in front of you.

9 ANTICIPATE WHAT THE QUERENT'S QUESTIONS MIGHT BE

Try and get a feel of the areas of greatest interest to them, and instead of letting them wait until you have finished a reading, use the enhancement technique of laying out additional cards on top of the basic Celtic Cross and other spreads in order to keep the reading flowing and informative.

10 THEMES

Go into the cards if they represent themes, not incidents or individuals. Find ways of applying the themes of the individual, not the other way round. Don't regard the cards as specific incidents, which necessarily must apply to the Querent. Again, it comes down to flexibility of approach and the need to avoid being mechanistic.

11 DON'T ALLOW YOUR READINGS TO BE NEGATIVE

An important point leads on from this last one, namely, that you should never allow your reading to be negative and depressing. Don't underestimate the force for good – you can be helping the Querent get their life together. And this doesn't just mean telling them 'good news' or by sitting there 'giving them hope'. That was the job of the soothsayer.

Your function is to help them draw up a map for themselves through which, firstly, they may understand where they are in their lives. Secondly, what is it that they have done which has created the effect – positive or negative – that they are currently experiencing. Thirdly, *how* can they go about redirecting their lives along a path which is more in accordance with what they are hoping to achieve.

It is a bit like seeing someone about to walk into a hole in the pavement. Rather than allow them to have an injury you would call out to them and draw their attention to the problem(s) you foresaw for them.

12 DON'T BE SCARY

Always be aware of the implications – moral and ethical – of what you are telling the other person. Try to be become more aware of your own 'blind spots' experientially and avoid giving your own prejudices free rein. Remember that what has been true for you might not be applicable to the person in front of you.

Become aware of the limitations of the Tarot. It is *not* some infallible oracle of the Gods. It is simply a set of pictures set down on pieces of paper. What we make of it is entirely up to us. Remember that any significance is what we assign to the objective reality.

13 THE HINT OR SUGGESTION OF ACTIVITY IN THE CARDS

As you look through a spread of Tarot cards, you will sometimes notice that some of the cards may begin to suggest movement or action in a very gentle way. This is a prompting for you to pay particular attention to those areas symbolized by the moving parts of the cards.

For example, you might notice that one of the figures in a card stands out in a certain way or that their hand is drawing something back, rather than presenting it.

Be sufficiently on your toes to deal with the 'hint' which your own intuition is picking up on in the life of the Querent, as expressed through the hint of movement or action in their cards. Another instance which some have noticed is in the Court cards, where sometimes a particular figure will be seen to be 'arriving', and in somebody else's spread, the same figure will be perceived as 'going', i.e. entering the Querent's life, or departing from it.

14 GETTING IT WRONG

You will only find yourself 'getting it wrong' if you make absolutely definitive statements about what you feel is taking place. If you find yourself halfway through a reading and *then* you start getting negative feedback from the Querent, try to backtrack to a point where you and the Querent had a consensus and build again from there, taking care to avoid letting your readership style fall into the same trap a second time. The main problem in this area is likely to be the trainee having an artificially high expectation of being a genius within the first few hours of training. The craft of Tarot is something which – hopefully – will be an ongoing experience with you for the rest of your life and not just a blip on the screen! You have a lot of time in which to learn and grow from one level to another.

15 CONSTANT PRACTICE

Reading the Tarot is rather like going to a gym. You have to keep it up and practise it constantly and consistently to really get anything from it at all. Don't be like those people who go to the gym once a month and still complain that they are getting nothing out of it. If you only do one reading a month you are not going to make anywhere near as much progress as if you do one reading a day.

It would be good for you to actually have a target number of readings. Have your own selected number of readings, but be sure to choose people who aren't going to turn your early attempts into a mockery. If you feel confident enough, you might even like to take your cards down to the local wine bar (with a friend or two in tow for support!) and start reading peoples' cards down there!

Be adventurous. You will be amazed at the positive response you create, not to mention the people that you come across that you wouldn't ordinarily meet. I have even known trainees meet their future marriage partners in this way!

16 USE THE CARDS AS FRONT PAGE HEADLINES

Remember that it is up to you to interact with the Querent and 'fill in' with a relevant storyline.

Allow the contrasting images to clash, remember that not everything will fit together in nice neat little antiseptic rectangles.

183

People's lives abound with contradictions and it is this – amongst other things – that the cards will pick up on!

17 USE YOUR IMAGINATION!

Don't just rattle off a mechanistic 'meaning' for the cards which have fallen in a Querent's spread. Try to 'see' just how these images might fit together. Let your imagination wander *freely*.

18 BRING IN ADDITIONAL CARDS ON TOP OF THE ORIGINAL LAYOUT

This is the technique of laying out additional cards *on top* of the original Celtic Cross as a means of getting more detailed information on a particular area of interest. Notice I say as much as you *can* and not as much as you like. This process is a powerful tool for really kick-starting the Celtic Cross into action, or any other spread which you may feel drawn to, for that matter.

19 WORK THROUGH THE SPREAD SYSTEMATICALLY

Don't dive off at too many tangents until you feel quite confident that you can find your way back!

20 TELL YOUR STORIES

As you move through the reading, let yourself slide into the role of bard. Let the images of the Tarot trigger your imagination and let the stories in the back of your mind float to the surface. They might be recollections of fairy-tales, stories from the Bible, tales from Greek or Indian mythology, whatever. But let them come forward and out into the reading. They might even be stories from your own personal experience. Again, don't bore the Querent by going on and on without purpose, but use your tales as a way of *enhancing* the meaning of particular cards and spicing up the reading itself. After you have gone into your story, bring the Querent back to the actual reading by touching the card which has acted as the trigger and by finding a way of linking that particular card with some of the surrounding cards.

21 DIFFERENT SPREADS

Some people feel that they have to be able to demonstrate all kinds of fancy-looking spreads to their Querent in order to be able to impress them with their competency.

Why? This is a misconception. The ultimate value of a reading is really in terms of a sharing of light, not a stagy, showy series of patterns which the cards can be shown to make on a table. By the same token, there is much to be said for becoming adept at moving fluidly from one spread to another, as the Querent's own energy and needs might suggest the formation of different patterns through which their lives may be more readily interpreted. We have already looked at a variety of different spreads, which I would like you to familiarize yourself with. This will form the basis on which you will build, over the next few months or years. You may even eventually like to experiment and work out a spread which is completely individual to yourself. This is completely OK, as long as you keep constant the meaning of each segment of the spread: e.g. this part represents the future; this part represents the past, etc.

The more you can personalize the entire experience, the better!

22 GET THE SETTING OF THE ROOM RIGHT BEFORE YOU START

If it helps you to have some classical music playing in the background, play it. If you like having crystals around while you are reading someone's cards, then do so, or maybe light a special lamp or candles. A word or warning about candles, though: be especially careful around them and never leave them burning when you are going out of the room for any length of time. Those fire elementals can be too playful when the human influence moves out of range even for a few moments!

23 RECORDING THE SESSION ON CASSETTE OR ALLOWING THE QUERENT TO TAKE NOTES

I have found that once you get used to having the cassette recorder on the table – it will take only a few readings at most – this is a wonderful way for your Querent to go over the session time and time again and thus derive much more benefit from the reading than if they had to rely solely on their own memory.

To a lesser or greater extent, we all have a selective listening band, and the cassette is an ideal way to enable the Querent to concentrate on your reading while in session.

The practice of note-taking has its pros and cons. On the plus side it enables the Querent to have a record of what their reading actually said to them and thus avoid forgetting important sections. On the minus side, it can at times interfere with the fluidity of the session, with the reader being distracted from focusing in on the cards. Some find that they are able to get used to this minor distraction quite easily, feeling that it is more than compensated for by the Querent having at the end of the reading something which they are then able to refer to.

But if you are going to use a cassette recorder, then get a good quality one. There is little so frustrating as running an absolutely first-rate reading, only to find that the recording which comes out is barely audible.

24 HELP

Remember that you are there to help, not hinder, the progress of the person in front of you. Remember that as a Tarot reader, you have a special responsibility. You can create wonderful karma for others – and yourself – if you remain true to the principles which have inspired you to learn this craft. There really is some kind of spirit watching over practitioners of this craft. Those who start to abuse their power, who become manipulative or cease to value the experience which they have entered into, will rapidly find that their interest in the subject wanes and find themselves on the outside of the craft.

25 SUMMING UP

In summing up at the end of a reading, bring out the main points – don't let the reading drag on without any sense of direction.

Remember that *you* are the taxi-driver and that you are in control of the reading. Some clients will want to keep the reading going on even after everything possible has been looked at. Don't let this happen. Gently, but firmly, draw the reading to a close after you feel that it is time to end it – that may be after, say, half an hour or 40 minutes, or possibly an hour.

It will always depend on so many variable factors. But it is *you* who will get the feeling that the time has come to close down.

And then you should.

26 BE YOURSELF

You don't have to 'become' anyone else in order to do an effective reading. Working with the Tarot is all about emphasizing your own individuality, rather than trying to live up to someone else's ideal. And don't bluff. If you don't see something there in someone's cards, don't feel pressurized into saying that you do. Some people will try to force you psychologically into telling them something which they wish to hear. They will respect you far more if you don't get into playing any of these games and simply stay in the truth of the whole thing.

12

Now About Those Cards You Can't Remember

Every trainee reader is going to have a problem remembering the meaning of some of the cards; or, at the very least, some of the cards are going to have a greater relevance than others at different times and at different stages in our lives.

But it's the ones which we have the greatest difficulty in learning and accessing which are big hints from the Tarot that we ought to be looking at how these issues are really blind spots in our lives.

In a sense, it is the cards which we have the greatest difficulty in accessing which have got the greatest message for us.

So, when you discover what your blind spots are, don't get huffed, but instead be thankful to the Tarot for having drawn your attention to what they are, because now you will become able to put some energy into resolving those very same issues.

You see, how we approach the Tarot is really a symbol of how we approach our own lives.

If someone approaches the Tarot with great fear and trepidation, chances are that that is how they are approaching most issues in their life.

If someone approaches the Tarot with hope and confidence, again it is an indication that this is the basic way that they approach their lives.

The Tarot is a great friend and will point out to you areas of your life which are in need of overhaul.

By surfacing as a card or as cards which you find at first difficult to relate to, it will highlight issues which you need to confront – and handle!

13

DOING THE SAME WITH PLAYING CARDS

Playing cards are the same as Tarot cards, except that they consist of the Minor Arcana only, and even then with just the Page, Queen and King, and no Knight.

They work as follows:

Earth	Coins	Diamonds
Air	Swords	Spades
Fire	Wands	Clubs
Water	Cups	Hearts

A brilliant exercise for remembering the cards really well is to go through a deck of ordinary playing cards and recall what is the associated picture in the Tarot. Just pick up the playing cards and sift through them at random.

Now shuffle the playing cards and go through them a dozen or so times, until you get it dead right. Then you will find yourself getting to know your Tarot cards really well.

Once you get the hang of that, start using the playing cards for spreads. Not only is this a real challenge and great fun, but your friends will be *really* impressed!

14

BRAINSTORMING THE
FOUR ELEMENTS

Here we have a set of exercises which are designed to enhance your personal link with the four elements.

The purpose of each is to give you further ideas as to what each of them represents, so that you can relate to them more fluidly and bring into your work with the Tarot the associations which each of them will give you.

Refer to these sheets as often as you like; you will find them a constant source of inspiration in your work as a reader over the coming years.

ELEMENTAL EXERCISES

In the Minor Arcana we have the four elements: Earth, Air, Fire and Water. The following exercises have been put together as a way of enhancing your ability to connect with those qualities. Remember that the titles of the four elements have not just a link with the physical elements, but with the emotional and spiritual qualities which they point towards.

The Tarot isn't just a divinatory device. Its main purpose is – and actually always was – to enable us to work with the images represented for greater spiritual growth, greater effectiveness as human beings. At this point we shall take a look at ways in which we can enhance *your* relationship with the elemental forces which are represented in the Minor Arcana.

Go through the exercises below, giving yourself a complete evening of uninterrupted time in which to 'soak yourself' with each of the elements.

Again, give yourself the full benefit of what you are going to experience by taking the time and trouble to write up your experiences afterwards. You probably won't feel like it at the time, but it will be an excellent grounding process for you to follow, forcing you to fully earth yourself at the end of each meditation.

The discipline of keeping a spiritual diary is an excellent way of objectifying what you experience, of being able to stand back and get a sense of perspective of what you are going through.

It may well be the case that you find you have a stronger affinity with one element than with another. Be conscious of your thoughts, emotions, reactions to each of the four elements as you work your way through.

You may also feel that you have a major problem in relating to one of the elements. For instance, you might have particular difficulty in concentrating on the evening when you are about to work through the meditation on the Earth element. Or there may be a series of interruptions in your household when you are trying to get down to the evening's meditation on the Water element. When this happens, you are being shown something about the nature of your own life. For example, in the latter case, the Tarot may be bringing up issues of an emotional nature for you to confront and get a resolution on. A feeling of boredom whilst concentrating on the Air element might be suggesting that it is better for you to go out and get some *air* into your system, by taking a long walk. And this feeling might be prevalent for quite some time before it finally subsides and allows you to get back to your work on the cards.

You see, what you are beginning to discover is that you are now entering the state of weaving the Tarot into aspects of your own personal life. And in connecting with the force of the Universe, of which the Tarot is a representation, you will begin to experience some certain and definite changes.

To live the Tarot isn't just the same thing as reading the cards. It's as different as living life and just reading about it in newspapers.

TRIGGERS FOR WORKING WITH THE EARTH ELEMENT

The Earth element is represented by the suit of Pentacles, also known as Coins and sometimes even as Disks. In ordinary playing cards, it is represented by the suit of diamonds, which is the most precious symbol of the creative energies of earth. Earth is feminine, it is receptive. In all ancient mythologies, it is represented as a goddess. Earth represents the physical body, the tangible world. It is through this dimension that all other spiritual forces represent themselves through manifestation. It is through the realm of Earth that karma is worked out. The Earth is rather like a factory, cracking, melting, crushing, recycling, transforming our wastes in its secret laboratories. Earth provides satisfaction for the physical senses: taste, hearing, touch, sight and smell.

To be able to function on a spiritual level, you must first be able to master the energies of Earth. It represents grounding and practicality. Lack of Earth will result in imbalance; too much will lead to sense-gratification, selfishness, lack of spiritual vision.

EXERCISES TO GET YOU IN TOUCH WITH EARTH

1. Go to a forest or woodland. Sit there and meditate on the changing seasons and how this might apply to your life.
2. Meditate on the Ace of Coins. Write down your thoughts.
3. Find your roots, centre yourself. Become more aware of your body, your strength.
4. Play with clay, sand, wood, crystals. Identify with their beauty.
5. Develop your own creativity. Learn how to make something. If you have knowledge of a craft, do something with it and experience afresh what you are doing as spiritual.

THE EARTH ELEMENT REFLECTED IN THE MAJOR ARCANA

The Empress	Venus – love and harmony	Mother, fertility
The Hierophant	Taurus – stability, tradition	Teacher, guru, mason
The Hermit	Virgo – care, caution	Critical, analytical
The Devil	Capricorn – achievements	Success, materialism
The World	Saturn – lessons, manifestation	Responsibilities

As you can see from the above, an excess or insufficiency of any one of the qualities of Earth can lead to problems in our lives. For example, too much adherence to tradition can prevent us from exercising our spontaneity in the face of new situations. On the other hand, complete disregard for our responsibilities would make us very selfish. In life, it is all a question of achieving a balance.

EXERCISE

There may be many other trigger words which you might like to add to those given above. Get a piece of paper and write them down. You may wish to keep a record of these additions and add to them as time goes on. Include them in your notes.

TRIGGERS FOR WORKING WITH THE AIR ELEMENT

The Air element is represented by the suit of Swords. In ordinary playing cards, it is shown as spades. Air is gaseous, and is composed of oxygen and nitrogen. It represents the mental body, the intellectual faculties. Air is rational, scientific. It shows us the way to know about something, through the exercise of the mind, through thinking things through, rather than just jumping to conclusions. It teaches us to become aware of our own prejudices and limiting thought-patterns. It connects with the value of deep-breathing, as a foundation for meditation and stress management.

Everything living in the universe breathes: trees, the stars, the oceans, even stones.

The Air element gives us the potential to identify and realize our goals. Too much Air can make people out of touch with their feelings, able to perform experiments on animals and even humans without any qualms. Too little Air can create difficulty in communication, religious fundamentalism, political intolerance.

EXERCISES TO GET YOU IN TOUCH WITH AIR

1. Go and sit down somewhere quietly by yourself and breathe deeply. Become aware of your own thoughts. Let all of those different thoughts run through your mind, without holding on to any or pushing away any others.
2. Sit down in front of a mirror and say something to yourself that you would like to see happen in your life or which you would like someone else to communicate to you.
3. Meditate on the Ace of Swords. Visualize yourself pulling such a sword out from an anvil. Look around and see what historical and/or mythological setting you find yourself in.

Write down your thoughts and add these to your file.

THE AIR ELEMENT REFLECTED IN THE MAJOR ARCANA

The Fool	Uranus – originality, eccentricity	Adventurous, unrestrained
The Magician	Mercury – communication, messages	Study, learning, languages
The Lovers	Gemini – duality, feeling 'linked' together	
Justice	Libra – balance, karma	The Law of Cause and Effect
The Star	Aquarius – humanitarian	Detached, visionary, unemotional

EXERCISE

Get yourself a pen and paper and add other triggers to the above list. Stretch your intellect, use your memory. Think of what might logically come into each category. Communicate what you discover either to yourself through your notes or to someone else through words.

TRIGGERS FOR WORKING WITH THE FIRE ELEMENT

The Fire element is represented by the suit of Wands, also known as Rods or Batons. In ordinary playing cards it is shown as clubs.

Fire is thought of as a masculine element. It directs, orders, gives light. The ultimate symbol of Fire is the Sun, which represents the Father principle, from which all planets have emerged.

In mythological stories, Fire is often represented as having been stolen from the Gods and brought down to Earth by a saviour figure, so that mankind could make use of it. The use of fire enabled mankind to keep wild animals at bay, to cook food and to work with metals. Prior to the advent of fire, mankind was very vulnerable against the forces of nature. Fire gives us warmth and represents hope. It seems to burn more brightly when arraigned against a gloomy background. Fire is the transformative element. With fire underneath it, a pan of water turns from its liquid state to vapour, as a lake or river evaporates similarly under the rays of the sun.

Fire has come to stand as a symbol of liberty, of conscience.

Fire needs to be strictly controlled, because of its own basic tendency to get out of hand. When this happens, it becomes destructive. In the form of lightning, it is a symbol of divine retribution and a warning to those who would commit evil. Too little Fire results in lack of enthusiasm, depression and apathy. Too much leads to wars, revolutions, oppression, burn-outs.

EXERCISES TO GET YOU IN TOUCH WITH FIRE

1. Go off by yourself and make a fire, starting from scratch.
   Become aware of each stage of its construction as symbolic.
2. Meditate on the Ace of Wands.
3. Meditate on what kind of world it would be without fire.

THE FIRE ELEMENT REFLECTED IN THE MAJOR ARCANA

The Emperor	Aries – leadership	The Conqueror, forceful, headstrong
Strength	Leo – pride	Kingly, knightly, large-scale
Temperance	Sagittarius – freedom	Expansive, optimistic, busy
The Tower	Mars – energy, action	Powerful, angry, unruly
The Sun	The Sun – growth	Father, example, purpose, generosity
Judgement	Pluto – powerful transformative energies	Strong drives, obsessions, the ability to transform

EXERCISE

Become aware of yourself in your moments of enthusiasm; how nothing seems difficult for you to overcome. Notice how easy it is for you to achieve your goals when you are interested in what you are doing. Learn how to expand your enthusiasm, to keep your own inner fire burning constantly. Become aware as to how this could enable you to overcome your own barriers and change your lifestyle.

TRIGGERS FOR WORKING WITH THE WATER ELEMENT

Water is represented in the Tarot as Cups or Chalices. In ordinary playing cards it is shown as hearts. Water is thought of as a feminine element. It is receptive, it dilutes and absorbs. It is associated with healing, with washing clean the wounds incurred in battle. It represents the world of feelings, emotions, sensations, desires; it gives us depth. Without these things, we become 'shallow'. Water is the most versatile of each of the elements, being able to assume any state: gas, liquid or solid. Water teaches us how to love and how to forgive. Without water, a piece of land becomes just a desert. Without emotions, our lives become similarly arid. Water purifies. It washes away negativity, both physically and on other levels. Physically, it cleanses out our bodies. Seekers of all ages have all had to undergo some process of purification in which water was the predominant symbol. It is the gateway to the higher dimensions. In the Arthurian legends, for example, it was the Lady of the Lake who presented the sword Excalibur to Arthur. It is the most powerful of all the elements. In the form of the great sea it is the mother of all living creatures, even we humans, who emerged from it onto land millions of years ago. The force of the raging sea is something which even earth cannot long hold back. It is the sea which erodes continents and builds them up in other places. It is the force of water which takes from one place and places somewhere else. All the ancient legends contain references to a time of a great flood.

Too much water will drown everything out. Too much emotion will lead to irrationality, escapism. Too little creates an emotional desert in which no growth or life can take place.

EXERCISES TO GET YOU IN TOUCH WITH WATER

1. Become more attentive to your feelings. Are you really in touch with them?
2. Meditate on the Ace of Cups. What is your response to whatever gets stirred up from this?
3. Let yourself be guided by your feelings towards people. Are you really spending enough time with the people you like and too much with those that you don't like? Why?

THE WATER ELEMENT REFLECTED IN THE MAJOR ARCANA

The High Priestess	The Moon – intuition	Subconscious, receptive, telepathic
The Chariot	Cancer – caring	Nurturing, mother, conception
Death	Scorpio – rebirth	Compulsions, obsessions, sexuality
The Hanged Man	Neptune – Water	Unselfish, self-sacrificing, submissive
The Moon	Pisces – sensitive	Secrets, responsive, impressions
The Wheel of Fortune	Jupiter – abundant	Tides, currents, flows, celebrations

EXERCISE

How do you feel about the emotions you go through each day? Become more in touch with your feelings. Be true to how you feel. Don't let guilt or other people's baggage come into the equation.

15
MEDITATION WITH
THE TAROT

USING THE TAROT CARDS AS DOORWAYS

Quite a pleasant way to get in touch with the force which a card may symbolize is to create a quiet time and space for yourself, preferably when you are alone, and to light up a candle and actually place the card that you want to meditate on, just by the side of it.

Allow yourself to 'step into the picture' and, as you do so, become conscious of what you are now wearing, of where you might be going, of what your new name might be.

Allow yourself to float for some time in this 'halfway world' of dream experience. While you are there look around to see if there is anything going on, maybe close to where you are standing. Maybe further away – over on the horizon, possibly. Notice whether there is anyone standing around. What is it that they are saying to you. Does a creature – a dog, a cat, a lion, a dragon, for example – come up to meet you?

What kind of dialogue might begin to develop now between the two or more of you? Do you see any writing on a wall?

When you do decide to 'come back', close an imaginary door behind you, just as a way of symbolically finishing your journey.

Keep a diary of your journeys, as a way of developing an overview of whatever is surfacing from your mind.

As your journeys develop, so will their level of complexity.

This is a technique long used by writers and mystics alike, for inspiration.

You will find it very helpful indeed in your Tarot studies to 'get into' the cards in this way. Meditation is really the art of entering different states of consciousness at will. You don't have to sit in any strange position or breathe in any unnatural way in order to do this – forget anything you might have seen in books on eastern yoga and mysticism. 'Entering' into the cards in this way will enable you to make a special connection with the character, or 'energy', of the card. It will trigger off a response somewhere within you, and create a resonance between you and the card. Thus, on quite a deep spiritual level, you will deepen your connection and enrich your association with each of the cards.

It is important to 'close off' after you have made your journey so that you are fully grounded and in a frame of mind to deal with the mundane realities of everyday life again. Meditation is not a form of mental escapism, after all.

1 THE KNIGHT OF SWORDS

You find yourself awakening on a field of mud, dressed in medieval garb (or the garb of some other historical time). It is cold and the wind is blowing strongly. From all around you, you hear the crash and din of men screaming, bugles blowing and horses whinnying. As your sight clears, you see that you are on the top of a hill and all around you huge armies are battling with one another.

Different coloured flags and pennants are flying, with a multitude of heraldic symbols upon them. As you stand upright, pulling yourself with every effort to your feet, you notice that a single horseman, with an outstretched arm bearing a sword has noticed you. With a fixed glare of determination in his eye, he begins to ride up the incline towards you. What do you do? Is he a friend come to help you get away from the scene, or is he a foe, coming to cut you down? *Continue the scenario from here …*

2 THE FOOL AND THE MAGICIAN (TAKEN TOGETHER)

You are a soldier/farmer/priest (choose your own occupation). You find yourself on an open road which winds into the distance. The day is hot, it is midsummer and the thirst for water is strong in your throat. You know that you have many more miles to travel before you are to arrive at your destination. You take a bend in the road and after about half an hour realize that you have never been down this road before. This thought strikes you as strange, as you have lived in this area for a number of years and thought you knew it quite well. Unexpectedly you spot a small country inn as you round the next bend. Great strong oak trees flank this establishment, providing shade for the small number of people who sit outside drinking and, as you can see more clearly now as you come closer, being entertained by the antics of a court jester and a magician. How these two people have come to meet up, you do not know, but you are pleasantly surprised at the cleverness of the magician's tricks, finding yourself quite unable to explain how he does it. The jester comes over to you now and says something to you … What does he say? How do you respond? What happens after that? Do you become their friend or does all this turn out to be an irrelevant encounter due to your earlier wrong turn in the road? Do you have a drink? Do you spend the night at the inn? Do you continue on your journey? Do you meet either or both or neither of these characters later on? *Continue the scenario from here …*

These are but two samples – your journey is for *you* to make! Get to work!

16

TWINNING

How did you get on with the Tarot Worksheets? I do hope that you haven't skipped over them, as getting through them does represent an important part of your learning process. Even if you have already worked through them, there's no harm in cycling through them again. I am a bit worried that your studies may have hit some sort of an impasse.

Some people start a study of a subject and then, bit by bit, their enthusiasm wanes. If you fall into this category, what I am going to suggest to you is what I suggest to all of my students when they get to this point, which is more often than you might think. And that is: get a twin.

The Tarot isn't like any other subject you have tried to learn, so you can't think that you can learn it in the way you have learned other subjects.

Only up to a point can it be learned on your own. Sooner or later you are going to have to come into contact with people to read for. The sooner you begin to link up with people who share your interest in this subject the better. The very essence of Tarot is that it brings people together. A very effective way to learn the Tarot is for you to find a twin, i.e. someone else who is also committed to learning. This person should ideally be known to you already. If it is a really old friend, so much the better.

The first thing you must do is sit down and work out a schedule with your twin in terms of when and where you are going to meet and for each of you to take it in turns to be teacher/student.

You might like to try a schedule of two hours at a time, spread over a month. Don't just get together and chatter, but have in mind a clear set of objectives for each training session.

For example, say we have two people – Bob and Stephanie – both of whom wish to learn the Tarot.

1st session: 1 September
    Time: 7–9 p.m.
    Place: Bob's
    Subject: Major and Minor Arcana familiarization, Suit of Coins,
      Suit of Swords – Basic meanings

2nd session: 8 September
    Time: 7–9 p.m.
    Place: Stephanie's
    Subject: Suit of Wands, Suit of Cups – Basic meanings

3rd Session: 14 October (Saturday afternoon)
    Time: 2–4 p.m.
    Place: Stephanie's
    Subject: Major Arcana – Basic meanings

4th Session: 21 October (Saturday afternoon)
    Time: 3–5 p.m.
    Place: Bob's
    Subject: Linking the cards together in trial spreads –
    Heightened Meanings

5th Session: 29 October (Sunday evening)
    Time: 6–8 p.m.
    Place: Stephanie's
    Subject: Invitation to friends to come over to act as guinea pigs
    in a social setting, where Bob and Stephanie can give readings
    in a supportive atmosphere. Here about eight or so friends can
    be invited, with Bob and Stephanie sitting in different rooms,
    set apart from the living room where the friends can congregate
    together.

Twinning is probably the most effective way of teaching any subject, but especially something like the Tarot. It will give you personally the responsibility to ensure that your twin is able to make progress in their studies and that they are able to demonstrate their knowledge. Remember that your role as somebody's twin is supportive and not punitive. Once your schedule with your twin is established, do please try to keep to it. Don't ring up 10 minutes before and cancel. It is quite a commitment to follow through on an agreed schedule, but if you do so I can definitely guarantee the results that you will reap. As you both progress in your schedule, you can monitor each other's progress in filling out the worksheets.

This will be the place where you will start functioning in your counselling role, because your twin will be showing you aspects of their life that may be highly confidential or at the very least have been quite traumatic. Remember that as a trainee, you will have to learn the art of helping people through traumatic experiences, of keeping confidences.

Also, you yourself will have to open up and reveal past experiences that you have been through.

A special bond of camaraderie is established between people when they train in this way. You may well find that you begin a friendship, a comradeship, that lasts a lifetime.

If you find, as your training progresses, that you suddenly can't stand your twin, recognize the importance of the teaching experience that you are going through. Stick with it. Don't blow the course just because of personality clashes. What you have embarked on is far too important for you to allow yourself to be blown off course by any self-sabotage or emotive reaction to somebody else's foibles. Remember, to work with the Tarot is to raise certain issues in your life: issues that you must at some point confront and overcome anyway!

By the same token, I don't want you to feel under any *compulsion* to find a twin. There are many ways in which we travel to our destinations and for some people the experience of twinning isn't the best way in which the Tarot can be mastered. But rather than staying blocked, could it be something for you to consider?

Different people learn in different ways and even if other things have arisen in your life since you commenced, recognize that this is probably something to be expected! After all, it is a life-changing experience to learn the Tarot. So please, let's keep the ball rolling!

17

ABOUT THE 'NEGATIVE' CARDS

The so-called 'negative' cards contain a lot in the way of guidance, showing people in simple ways how they can begin to go about helping others to improve their lives. Life is not all sweetness and light. Sometimes we have to confront and overcome limitations, bad things, the unpleasant. The three really big cards in the Tarot which enable us to do that are:

Death
The Devil
The Tower

Implicit in the meanings which you have already for these cards is powerful guidance. Unfortunately, irresponsible readers (or just the untrained) have succeeded in scaring the life out of people by giving them misleading meanings when these cards have come up. So remember that other people – when they see these cards come up – probably need a helping hand in coming to terms with certain problems which haven't necessarily been resolved as yet.

Some people have difficulty in understanding the difference between these three cards, anyway. The difference is best explained in the following analogy.

Death – 'The clearing away of negative influences' – someone else comes along and clears the table for you.
The Devil – 'Don't let your own negativity hold you back' – you have to clear the table yourself.
The Tower – 'The need to build on solid foundations' – you have to make sure the table is solid and not liable to collapse.

You can think of it along these lines!

18

USE A TAPE RECORDER

In order to get your technique polished up a bit, set up a tape recorder and start doing readings for imaginary friends, acquaintances, relatives. Anticipate the kinds of questions which they would ask. Let your imagination have free rein. No one is going to overhear you, so don't feel embarrassed. Let the tape run, and record your readings for them. Afterwards you can play it back and you will be pleasantly surprised at how professional it sounds. Quite a few people are also surprised at how their voices sound when they first hear it played back on a cassette. Just give yourself space to get through this one, and then go beyond it. You don't have to keep the tapes, necessarily. Record something else over them afterwards. After all, you are just using them to enhance your readership technique.

See also 'Practical Tarot Guidelines', tip number 23 (page 186).

19

How to Avoid Depletion

As you start to do readings on friends and, when you feel yourself ready, friends of friends, you will sometimes have need of a 'barrier' between yourself and the person in front of you. This barrier is an imaginary one, in which you visualize a glass partition between yourself and your client. Otherwise you can quite easily start to feel drained, even in a short space of time.

You won't need this with all of your clients, but you most definitely will with some. As soon as you start feeling your energy running down dramatically, use this technique.

With some clients, though, you will have to use quite the opposite technique to help them open up sufficiently to allow you as the reader to 'get in there' and do your job.

Here, the visualization is to create a bubble, say of a warm, glowing pink or rose radiance, around both yourself and your client. This technique I have found particularly useful in helping clients to talk about traumatic experiences, guilt, lack of self-worth, etc. There is no one 'correct' visualization; for some you might like to visualize the presence of an angel or a blue circle. But it is a good idea to look around in your mind and find something along these lines that you are comfortable with.

After a reading, it is also quite a good idea to 'earth' yourself, by standing up, moving the body about, touching the four walls in the room, stretching forward, bending, having a drink.

It is more important than you might think to actually activate the physical body, or at the very least one of the five physical senses.

It is also important to recognize that although you are now able to identify problems in people's lives and suggest remedies, you cannot function as a crusader and force them to do as you think they should.

Remember that your clients will like to think about what you have told them in their readings and that they aren't all going to rush out and change their lives overnight.

So you really have to accept that for some people it is going to take a while for them to be ready to discard something that is holding them back, and embrace the change.

Don't let it become frustrating. Recognize that we are all growing at our own rate of development. Accept. You have played your part as their reader, as their guide, as their confidante. Now the rest is up to them.

Psychically, a very helpful meditation I have used is to surround myself with white or even blue light, starting in a nimbus around the top of the head and moving down over the shoulders, eventually encasing the entire body in a tower of light. You don't have to make a big thing out of this. Just let it be a little space in your mind which you are able to slide into gently, and then after a few moments, slide back out of, back into the world of everyday reality.

As with any meditation, the more you practise this in nice, easy stages, the more easily you will incorporate the technique into your 'repertoire' of psychic procedures. And the more you will reap the benefits of a heightened energy level.

Some people may feel comfortable starting a reading with a prayer or with a meditation, either on your own or with the person whose cards you are going to read. If this feels right to you, you might even care to think of burning some essential oils before and during the reading and of using candlelight as a way of enhancing the overall effect.

One meditation which you will find extremely powerful is to visualize yourself doing a reading for someone as you drift off to sleep. This way you will programme your subconscious to be able to do readings with very little effort on the part of your conscious mind. You can change the Querent each night. One night you might like to have a stranger there in front of you; the next night you might well choose to have a relative or friend. Visualize the person shuffling the cards and handing them back to you. See the cards there on the small table in front of you and let the images on the cards be clear. As you go through the reading, see the positive effect your words are having on the other person. With someone who you know needs to be told something specific, or consoled, or given guidance, let them receive it in this way. See them thanking you for your time, etc, at the end of your reading. This is a very potent way of giving yourself the inner confidence to be able to do readings 'live'. As you drift off to sleep your subconscious mind will take over the image and translate it into its own memory circuits for future use.

With all of these practices, you will find what is most appropriate for yourself by actually experimenting, just as you will find that your own requirements will undergo change as well.

20

WHERE TO GO
FROM HERE

Very well done on getting this far with your training programme!
Now, the next thing for you to do is announce to your friends that
you are available for readings.

Organize for them to come round one evening and put you to
the test. Tell them to bring a bottle of wine with them, or at least
something to drink, and to bring a friend or two.

You seriously need an event such as this in order to give yourself
the confidence with which you can read anybody's cards.

When they turn up, put yourself in a side room and, one by
one, start reading their cards.

Be courageous and have a go at it! If it doesn't all work out at first,
don't get despondent. Remember, Rome wasn't built in a day. Any

growth process takes place over a period of time. But to be frank, I think that you will be amazed at how well you will do.

Just take your time and allow yourself the time to apply what you have learned. You don't have to present yourself in any glorified light. Your friends will be aware that you have just completed a study programme and won't expect miracles. Don't forget to thank them as well, for allowing themselves to be used as guinea pigs in this way.

Without an event such as this you will never be completely 'cooked'.

Your next training step after this is to get through a certain preselected number of readings.

Rather than me giving you a definite number of readings to get through, I would suggest that you set for yourself a rough figure and then make a point of aiming for that amount – because it is by doing, not thinking about doing, that you will see how everything fits together and continue to learn. I would emphasize this far more than simply reading other people's books on the subject.

There have been some marvellous contributions to Tarot literature, but you will get far more from the Tarot by emphasizing your own 'doing' than by looking at the theory. Save the other books for when you are about halfway through your target number of readings.

Be conscious of the impact which you are having on the Querent, on the quality of the reading. Be sensitive to the Querent's needs, and to the response you are getting to your reading. It's not just in churning out readings that you will develop your style.

Spend as much time as you feel able to, without allowing yourself to get exhausted: something which can happen without you realizing it at the time!

You might find it useful to keep a diary of what happens in these readings: mistakes you make; things you come to realize; wins; gains. You could also record in your diary how other, seemingly unconnected changes start taking place in your own personal universe. After the rest of your fixed number of readings you will be seeing things in a very different light. Your readership style will have undergone major changes, as you continuously blend your life with the mystical force of the Tarot and make it increasingly your own.

You may well change the deck you are working with, or you may find yourself working with different decks for different reasons. Or using different spreads. Or using different meanings for cards other than those which you first started out with.

It is important to number the readings as you go along. When you get to the end of your selected number of readings, it will be a major milestone for you – in some way! The other thing to remember is – of course – that you don't fall into the trap of thinking that you have arrived at your final destination spiritually.

It is important that you allow yourself to continue to learn from others, because as you are now outflowing more, so you will be receiving more information about other spiritual practices as well.

The Tarot training isn't the end of your learning process, but rather a milestone in your journey!

Please use the Knowledge well.

APPENDIX

As your association with the Tarot develops, you will increasingly get little flashes of inspiration about the person in front of you that have nothing to do with the standard meaning of the cards which they might have drawn in a reading. For example, you might get an impression that they spent some time travelling in Africa, that their girlfriend is German, or that they've just invented something. Small things, but if you bring them into the reading they will make it far more personal, and far more relevant, to the Querent.

Don't get anxious about tapping into this stuff though; it will come of its own accord.

The Tarot is marvellous in its role of helping the Querent locate where their problems might lie and in determining what they can do to solve them. The great thing about the Tarot is that it can allow two complete strangers to come together and look philosophically at their lives. If you tap into something that is upsetting for the Querent, remember that you can pull them through it – pull, that is, but not push.

In a reading, of course, you can ask some questions just to know how to make the cards fit into the Querent's life. But don't start asking dozens of questions; that's not what a reading is about.

Remember also that the cards very rarely – if ever – make definitive statements about what the future holds. They can only give possibilities, suggestions. Ultimately, it's all down to personal interpretation.

While you continue to learn the Tarot, you can certainly help a lot of people along the way and make some great friendships while you're at it.

CODE OF TAROT
READERSHIP

Now that you have completed this course in Tarot readership, you might feel able to commit yourself by signing the following ethical code.

As a Tarot reader, I pledge myself to the Code of Tarot for the good of all:

1. to use the Tarot to the best of my ability to help my family and friends, groups and other human beings;
2. to refuse to accept for readings anyone I feel cannot benefit from such, and to do readings only for those who want them and whom I feel might benefit from such;
3. to set an example of the effectiveness and wisdom of Tarot in my personal life;
4. to do what I can – however small – to help this world become a saner, better place.

Name... Date ....

Signature..

Witnessed by...

BIBLIOGRAPHY

I said at the beginning of this training programme that you *weren't* to read around the subject in other books. Because if you *had* done so, you would have deluged yourself with dozens of different influences, all conflicting with one another.

Now that you are actually relatively literate – from a Tarot point of view – it would be unrealistic to seal yourself off from all of the other influences which the various writers and creators of different decks have to offer you. At this point in your development you will now be able to get 10 times as much out of those other books than if you had tried to use them before. There are some brilliant books on the subject, but to get anything out of them you have to be relatively familiar with the language of symbols to start with. Hunt around and have a look for yourself. It's all about taking what is relevant to you personally and disregarding the rest. You're going to have to work it into your own personal equation.

I am recommending some books here, not because they are the most 'definitive' in the field, but because I think they offer some interesting perspectives. Have fun here, but don't forget: don't let someone else's theory become a substitute for your own direct experience of Tarot reading!

The Encyclopaedia of Tarot, Volumes 1, 2, and 3, by Stuart Kaplan. A masterful creation, encompassing the history of Tarot, mystical background of the cards and a review of hundreds of decks, some publicly available, some not.

The Mythic Tarot, by Juliet Sharman-Burke and Liz Greene. Re-establishing the links between the Tarot images and the ancient legends of Gods, Goddesses, heroes and anti-heroes.

Living the Tarot, by Amber Jayanti. Beautiful teachings through the Major Arcana, by a very illuminated lady.

The Tarot Handbook, by Angeles Arrien. Some dazzling suggestions for different interpretations and different layouts.

The Fruits of the Tree of Life, by Omraan Mikhael Aivanhov.
A glorious unveiling of the Tree of Life by a man who was a
Master, not just a teacher.

Tarot: Mirror of the Soul, by Gerd Ziegler. Using the Tarot to look
within and as affirmations for personal change.

The Element Tarot Handbook, by Naomi Ozaniec. Introduction to
Hebrew Letters and numerology.

The Shining Paths, by Dolores Ashcroft-Nowicki. An experiential
journey through the Tree of Life.

About the Author

Terry Donaldson is a down-to-earth mystic who has been living, breathing, studying, consulting with and teaching the Tarot for 20 years.

He is also an experienced astrologer and professional Tarot reader.

Along with Peter Pracownik, who also painted the cards and Mike Fitzgerald the game creator, he is a co-creator of 'Wyvern, the Game of Dragons, Dragon-Slayers and Treasure', a trading card game and book set based on mythology, in which the players activate dragons, gods, goddesses, witches and heroes in a struggle of contending empires. With Peter he has also co-created the Dragon Tarot deck, in which the symbolism of dragon legends from every historical epoch and from every corner of the globe has been drawn together. Terry is currently working on a dragon encyclopaedia, and a set of magical tales in novel and film format. He is also author of *Principles of Tarot* published by HarperCollins, and appears regularly on radio and television.

Terry is Founder and Director of the London Tarot Centre where he and his wife Evelyne teach the tarot to a high degree of excellence, through seminars, workshops, correspondence courses, and one-to-one tutorials. It is also possible to arrange to have tarot and/or astrological readings from him by contacting the Centre.

If you are at all interested in the sound of all this, you are welcome to make contact at the London Tarot Centre, either by phoning or by writing:

The London Tarot Centre,
25, Gisburn Road,
Crouch End, London, N8 7BS
Tel: 0181 340-3788

If phoning from outside the UK, please use the international code first.

FURTHER CONTACTS

Thorsons, HarperCollins*Publishers*, 77–85 Fulham Palace Road, London, W6 8JB, England. Tel: 0181 741 7070.
(Thorsons publish a very wide range of tarot decks and books, as well as books on personal development in general, and you should definitely phone in for a catalogue.)

TAROT DECKS, BOOKS AND SUPPLIES OF 'WYVERN, THE GAME OF DRAGONS, DRAGON-SLAYERS AND TREASURE'
(Again, just phone of fax for a catalogue.)

U.S. Games Inc., 179 Ludlow Street, CT06902, USA.
Tel: 001 2303 353 8400. Fax: 001 203 353 8431.

David Westnedge, 5 Ferrier Street, London, SW18, England.
Tel: 0181 871 2654.
(For tarot supplies and copies of the game 'Wyvern, the Game of Dragons, Dragon-Slayers and Treasure'.)

Mysteries, 9/11 Monmouth Street, Covent Garden, London, WC2H 9DH, England. Tel: 0171 240 3688.
(For tarot decks, books, supplies, as well as tarot courses and readings. This shop is well worth a visit for those visiting London, as well as those already living there.)

THE MIND BODY SPIRIT FESTIVAL (FOR INTERNATIONAL CONTACTS, FESTIVALS ETC.)
IN THE UK: **New Life Designs,** 170 Camden Hill Road, London, W8 7AS. Tel: 0181 938 3788. Fax: 0171 723 7256.

IN AUSTRALIA: **New Life Promotions,** Loched Bag 19, Pyrmont, NSW 2009. Tel: 0061 2 552 6833. Fax: 0061 2 566 2354.